FIVE HOUSES

1976-1986

ANTHONY AMES

ARCHITECT

FIVE HOUSES

1976-1986

ANTHONY AMES
ARCHITECT

INTRODUCTION
BY
THOMAS SCHUMACHER

POSTSCRIPT
BY
RICHARD MEIER

PRINCETON ARCHITECTURAL PRESS

Published in the United States of America in 1987
by
Princeton Architectural Press
2 Research Way
Princeton, NJ 08540

LC: 87-25727
ISBN: 0-910413-41-X (cloth)
ISBN: 0-910413-29-0 (paper)

FOR

ECETRA
AND
THE DUCKLINGS

CONTENTS

INTRODUCTION

"There are innovators and there are continuators. Innovators are Brunelleschi, Corbu, Mies, Wright. And then there are continuators like Peruzzi, Pei, you or me."

John Hejduk, to Cornell University Students, 1963

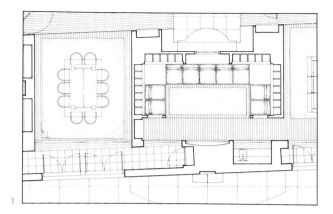

Anthony Ames is a 'continuator' architect. He is unabashedly so; he enjoys the role; and he has mastered a 'received' style of architecture. That style is the 'International Style,' the 'Modern-Movement Style,' the 'Machine Style,' the 'White Architecture of the Twenties' (Reyner Banham's term for the avant-garde of the 20's) or, if you will, the 'International Style' revived.

But Ames has not simply revived the architecture of the twenties and thirties; he is reviving the twenties-revival of the early seventies, the architecture of Graves, Meier, Rossi, Eisenman. This may appear to be third-hand eclecticism, indeed. But what Ames' architecture exposes (among other things) is our century's vastly over-emphasized premium on the sort of creativity that 'starts from scratch.' Unfortunately, that kind of creativity has produced things like boomerang-shaped coffee tables, paintings on velvet, and a self-assertive, anti-contextual architecture.

Instead, Ames' attentive and arduous exploration of a few simple themes, coupled with his careful attention to detail and source material, has made his houses object-lessons for the development of modern and post-modern ideas of spatial organization and formal manipulation. His work follows in the tradition of a Morandi or an Asplund (an acknowledged influence) displaying an involvement in a particular *genre* of objects and ideas, and playing with them, worrying them, creating an *oeuvre* that is both stylistically consistent as well as elegant and expressive. Other architects' names also come to mind: Cram, Dudok, Rainaldi, Lescaze. They are architects, like Ames, who on first inspection seem to be at the end of a tradition, but upon further notice, are in the thick of it, enlarging and expanding our perceptions and appreciation of an architectural system. Composers like Rachmaninoff also come to mind. His work seems so completely 19th century, yet he lived until the 1940's.

Ames, who resembles these artists, also works like a filmmaker, quoting from other films and thereby paying homage to past masters. (In this regard, one thinks of the *Potemkin* baby carriage in *Brazil*, or a quotation from *A Corner in Wheat* in *Witness*). These quotations are used as emblems of identification, such as the

Fig. 1 Hulse Residence: Detail of First Floor, Plan, 1985.

12

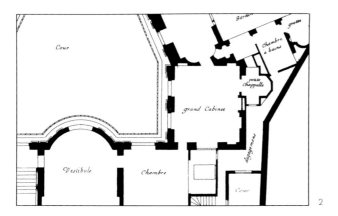

2

"Corbu" eyeglasses and hat in the VILLA CHANG, the Corbu car in the garage in the GARDEN PAVILION, or the "Krier" drapery in the HOUSE IN MISSISSIPPI. (This last house also contains various Corbu references, including a quotation from the Maison Cook: the figurine on the shelf.) The quotations supplement other levels of interpretation and re-interpretation.

Many of the references are subtle, by way of analogy rather than metaphor. Among these analogies is the idea of formal type. The idea is seen in Ames' work in how some of the plans (VILLA CHANG and the HULSE RESIDENCE, for example) recall the semi-detached row-house of the Eastern States. In the HULSE RESI-DENCE, the solid wall of the entry and stair zone becomes the ghosted party-wall of the semi-detached house, complete with empty window-holes, as if the house had been cleaved from its neighbor and is now awaiting its glazing.

A consistent parti, one that distinguishes an edge-circulation zone relating spaces having their own *enfilade* connections, appears in all the buildings presented in this collection. The distributive-functional clarity of these plans is reminiscent of the architecture of Richard Meier who is a significant influence on Ames. Circulation and repose, *poche* and *mosaic*, served and servant spaces, are all clearly articulated. In the HULSE RESIDENCE further elaboration on the theme of center versus edge occurs. Here the vertical circulation zone is pulled out of the volume, and is matched by a horizontal circulation zone *within* the volume. In addition, the rotated volume (another pervasive theme in Ames' work) has permitted an interesting variation on edge-circulation from the 'servant' space of the kitchen to the 'served' space of the dining room to occupy the thickened *poche*. The HULSE RESI-DENCE plan (like the other Ames plans in this book) thus presents a modern version of the *degagement* of the French Hotel,[1] (Figures 1, 2) using free-flowing space rather than the doors and cubicles of its traditional model. This 'occupiable *poche*' is a hallmark of Ames' plans and spatial experiences.

How the plan rotation and the occupiable *poche* work together is the essence of Ames' planning. In the GARDEN PAVILION, a combination of source references, architectural models used as a kind of architectural heuristic (literally to solve planning prob-lems), together with a plan rotation and occupiable *poche*, make for a dynamic spatial system. In this building the basic formal references are Corbusian. But the rotation in the plan comes not from Corbu, but from the Juan Gris painting compositions adapted by Colin Rowe and his Urban Design students of the six-ties and seventies, (another influence well recognized by Ames.

13

See Foreword.) Those projects showed an interest in edge relief in addition to the rotated composition. They pushed both the circulation and the eye to the edge of the composition. When converted into an architectural promenade, the result is only partly Corbusian. It is also reminiscent of the architectural promenades of Terragni's Casa del Floricoltore of 1936 (figure 3) and the Danteum project of 1938. In an early version of the GARDEN PAVILION (figure 4) we are led up the stairs along the long wall, led on by the light coming through the end window, extending our experience (like the glassless window at the top of the sequence in the Villa Savoye). In the built version the exterior stair has been rotated one hundred, eighty degrees for pragmatic reasons. But where Le Corbusier used curved objects in a neutral grid to drag us forward, and where Terragni used the shifted-rectangle in plan to create circulation zones, Ames rotates the interior volume in the plan to lead us down his promenade path. Like the rotation in the plan of the HULSE RESIDENCE (a significantly less dramatic shift) the rotation at the GARDEN PAVILION creates an occupiable *poche* along with an inflection that pulls us into the furthest recesses of the space. In all of these houses, then, the *degagement* that provides transition spaces without literal vestibules, is produced by rotation as compared to Terragni's displacement and Blondel's (and others') 'thickening' of the wall zone.

In this way Ames has achieved what many other architects who have embraced the 'poche plan' have also achieved: spatial hierarchy and perceptual thickness in walls that are otherwise hollow. But he has achieved these effects without having to eschew modern esthetics. No mean feat.

Nor has Ames abandoned the commitment to craft that was the hallmark of some of the architects of the modern movement. The drawings in this book are somewhat misleading in that respect. They show an apparent disdain for the literal incarnation of the building. But this initial reading should not be laid at Ames' feet. It is rather the fault of those architects who use the same conventions of drawing and who themselves are disdainful of the craft of architecture. Rather, for Ames, the precision of the drawing is reflected in a precision in the built work. The quality of the materials in the finished buildings is not forecast in the drawings, which are icons of ideas that, while contained in the buildings, are not complete indicators of all the ideas in the architecture. Many of Ames' buildings are clad in whitewashed brick. The textural effect, then, may be likened to that of certain Mondriaan paintings, where the surface of the paint mitigates the abstraction of the forms and colors. The walls of Ames' buildings also look better than stucco when the paint begins to peel. These buildings tread

14

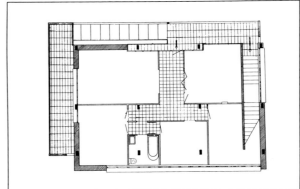

3

Fig. 3 Giuseppe Terragni: Casa del Floricoltore, Rebbio, Italy, Plan, 1935-37.

INTRODUCTION

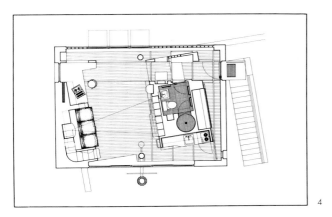

4

Fig. 4 Garden Pavilion: First Scheme, Plan, 1982.

the fine line between materialism and idealism. Ames is not in either camp in these matters. He pits the concrete against the abstract, like Corbusier and Terragni, whose work adheres to a physical, as well as metaphysical, reality. This is why it is so important for Ames to build his projects.

Thomas Schumacher
College Park, Maryland
1986

1. See Etlin, R. "Les Dedans: J. F. Blondel and the System of the Home," *Gazette des Beaux-Art*, April, 1978. See also, Dennis, Michael, *Court and Garden*, MIT Press, Cambridge, 1986.

The following projects are not presented as proposals for the method of architecture, but rather as a method for an architecture. Their representation is not offered as polemic, but rather as exploration.

In all of the projects, except the first, the Hulse Pavilion,[1] I have made similar assumptions about architecture and urban design, that when applied in a specific manner, form a technique, or method, for creating architectural form, space, and order. For example, rotation and superimposition serve as planning devices that permit certain conditions to exist in plan, and ultimately in three dimensions. As in Val Warke's competition entry for a museum in Dusseldorf (figure 5), the rotations and superimpositions found within the plan are founded upon two separate orthogonal systems such that the pattern generated by one system is superimposed on, and informed by, the pattern generated by the second system. The resulting plan is charged with a dynamism, or tension, that would not exist otherwise because we are asked to "read" both systems simultaneously. "As in the Cubist painting, when the organizational geometries do not reside in the objects themselves, the possibilities of combining various buildings within a system of order, which attributes to each piece a bit of the organization, become almost infinite."[2] By contrast, Paul Letarouilly's engravings of the Vatican (figure 6) illustrate a different conception of rotation. Instead of systems or overlapping patterns that create a transparency, discrete bodies collide, resulting in non-orthogonal adjacencies. The area of collision between both bodies is *poche*, a dense, thickened wall that allows the integrity of both spaces to remain intact.

The distinction between 'Modern' and 'Pre-Modern' (or as Michael Dennis has observed, Pre-Industrial or Pre-Enlightenment)[3] space has been described as one of opposing traditions.[4] Pre-Modern space is carved, anthropomorphic, 'objectified,' as in the Nolli Plan of Rome (figure 7), and Modern space, as in Le Corbusier's Plan Voison of Paris (figure 8) is continuous, infinite, boundless. The relationship between building and datum in the Pre-Modern tradition becomes a relationship between figure and ground, and the relationship between building and datum in the Modern tradition becomes a relationship between object and field. For example, the Uffizi Gallery (figure 9) by Vasari, as Fred Koetter and Colin Rowe have described[5] defines the exterior space that it circumscribes, and it merges with the existing fabric of Florence. The Unite d'Habitation (figure 10) by Le Corbusier floats above a non-differentiated and uninterrupted plane, serving to reinforce the notion that space is infinite, immeasurable, sempiternal. At a smaller scale, the difference between the Villa Madama (figure 11) by Raphael and Giulio Romano, and the house for the 1931 Berlin

16

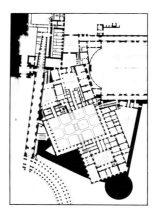

5, 6

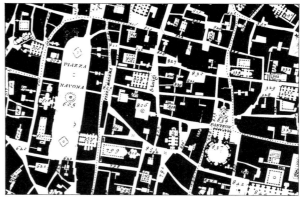

7

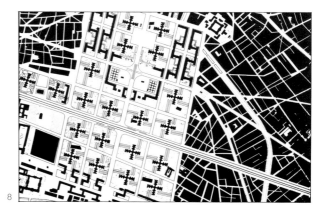

8

Fig. 5 Val Warke: Dusseldorf Competition Entry, Plan, 1975.
Fig. 6 Pontifical Palace, Vatican City, Italy, Detail of Ground Floor Plan, 1882.
Fig. 7 Giovanni Battista Nolli: Rome, Italy, Plan, 1748.
Fig. 8 Le Corbusier: Plan Voisin, Paris, France, 1925.

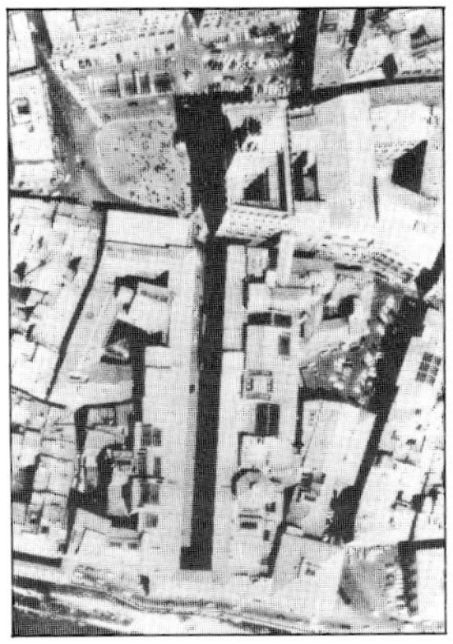

9, 10

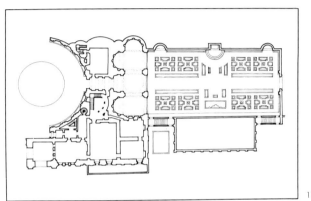

11

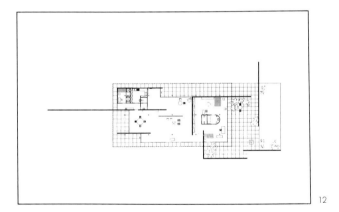

12

Fig. 9 *Giorgio Vasari: The Uffizi, Florence, Italy, Aerial View, 1559.*
Fig. 10 *Le Corbusier: Unite d'Habitation, Marseilles, France, Aerial View, 1946.*
Fig. 11 *Raphael and Giulio Romano: Villa Madama, Rome, Italy, Plan, 1516.*
Fig. 12 *Mies van der Rohe: House for Berlin Building Exhibition, Berlin, Germany, Plan, 1931.*

Building Exhibition (figure 12) by Mies van der Rohe illustrates the difference between Modern and Pre-Modern space. In the Villa Madama, rooms are contained, defined, and carved, becoming Platonic voids that, by virtue of the articulated poche defining them, appear as Platonic solids. In Mies' house, space is undifferentiated and formless, continuous and an infinite 'given' for the objects (service elements) that float in this continuous void.

That the Modern tradition in the modern city has absorbed the corporeal presence of the Pre-Modern tradition into an ever widening black hole, is a dilemma we are now forced to confront. However, as has been wisely studied and documented[6] it is possible to acknowledge these traditions by simultaneously making use of each. As in the case of precedents that have already revealed such enlightenment[7] the church of Sant'Agnese in the Piazza Navona in Rome (figure 13) by Borromini, is both an object and a space definer because of its centralized plan, and the articulation of the frontal wall facing the piazza. This wall, because of its thickness and profile, is a mediator between two different kinds of space; outside and inside, autonomous and static centralized space and the directional space of the rectangular piazza, requiring the front of Sant'Agnese to reinforce the 'wall' of the piazza. The condition to be found in the north pier of Sant'Agnese illustrates another enlightened possibility to be explored in the development of a coexistence of Modern and Pre-Modern space and has been observed by Steven Peterson[8] Poche has been typically understood as the 'area in-between,' the thickness of a wall, that separates and independently describes the space on either side. However in the north pier of Sant'Agnese the poche becomes occupied. Peterson also describes the work of Sir John Soane, who in his house at Lincoln's Inn Fields (figures 14, 15) demonstrates a clearer understanding of this possibility, and designs an architecture that begins to occupy the wall. As in the case of the thick habitable wall along the front facade of his house and between the parlor and the living room, one experiences both a sense of room,and a sense of uninterrupted continuity as spaces flow together.

Another dichotomy, illustrative of the difference between Modern and Pre-Modern space, that might be fused for a multifarious set of spatial consequences is the definition of center. In a plan of a Pre-Modern castle (figure 16), the service elements as well as different kinds of rooms occupy the poche[9] However, the hierarchical difference between the central space and those spaces surrounding it, insure the reading of the center as most important. In fact, by virtue of the independence of these spaces, mediated by poche, space becomes very important. On the other hand, in Mies'

17

project for a fifty foot square house (figure 17), the definition of center becomes the difference between the massiveness of the service core relative to the undefined and continuous space surrounding it. The transparency of wall here is intended to dematerialize it, unifying inside and outside. The plinth on which it sits, and the roof plane, are the only record of object, however anonymous. Center in this case has nothing to do with 'place-making,' but rather with the celebration of function, however abstract.

The simultaneous presence of a defined and dense center, and of center as void, would then become an opportunity to create an ambiguous reading of "sense of place," if placemaking can be associated with closure. In *Forest of Symbols* Victor Turner describes this condition as "liminal," a transition between states. "Undoing, dissolution, decomposition are accompanied by processes of growth, transformation and a reformation of old elements in new patterns. It is interesting to note how, by the principle of economy of symbolic reference, logically antithetical processes of death and growth may be represented by the same tokens...This coincidence of opposite processes and notions in a single representation characterizes the particular unity of the liminal: that which is neither this nor that, and yet both."[10] It is in the sense of orientation through hierarchy and symmetry, that the center as void was and is powerful spatially, and it is in the stimulation of the edges, the transposition of stasis to movement, that the Modern dense center is significant. When both are allowed to coexist in a manner that subtly applies both these phenomena, we can enjoy a sense of closure and psychological 'rest,' and a sense of open-endedness and continuity with the exterior environment. Ultimately, the experience of architectural space—Pre-Modern (figure 18) and Modern (figure 19) is heightened through the juxtaposition and simultaneous manifestation of the positive qualities of each.

Different evolutions of poche as principle, articulated by Peterson, Dennis, and others provide the method for achieving the simultaneity of 'solid' and 'void' and in a range of levels that allow for the development of different scales of experience. As Peterson writes:

"The architecture of the wall, of negative space, can incorporate another world of intimacy, emotion, and memory. It can contain places which are the equivalent of the attics and basements. Alcoves, window seats, inglenooks, hidden panels and secret passages, can be carved from the 'solid.' The space of the walls can provide new mystery, illusion and surprise."[11]

All the above references have informed the work presented here, but none of these works are direct applications of these allusions and it is with consideration that I present the quotations above as

18

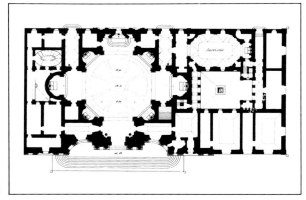

13

14

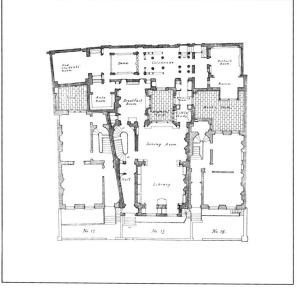

15

Fig. 13 Borromini: S. Agnese and Collegio Innocenziano, Rome, Italy, Plan, 1657.
Fig. 14 Sir John Soane's House: The Dining Room, London, England, seen from the Library, 1812.
Fig. 15 Sir John Soane's House, London, England, Plan, 1812.

FOREWORD

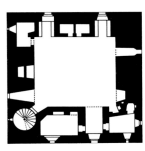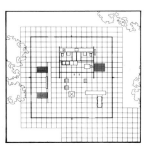

16, 17

18

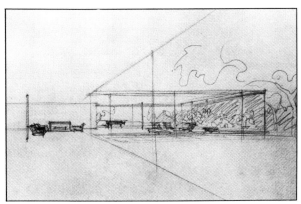

19

a forward to the work to follow. Each project embodies some or all of these principles, without positing any of them as unique solutions; rather, they are points of departure for a series of investigations that are not linear in development, nor conclusive as a set. Each project, beginning with a small pavilion completed about a decade ago, has only borne more to investigate.

Notes
1. The first project is based on a Modern aesthetic where the grid has been casually layered in the establishment of an order. Although it lacks the considerations that the others share, it is not wholly dissimilar, and it shares the site with the final project presented here.
2. Schumacher, Thomas, "Contextualism: Urban Ideals and Deformations," *Casabella* 104, 1971, p. 87.
3. Dennis, Michael, "Architecture and the Post-Modern City," *The Cornell Journal of Architecture*, Fall 1981, Rizzoli p. 48.
4. Schumacher describes, at some length, these differences at urban level in the article cited above, and attributes much of his discussion to Colin Rowe's work with graduate students at Cornell between the years 1963 to 1971. Steven Peterson discusses the differences between 'space' and 'anti-space' in an article entitled "Space and Anti-Space" in *The Harvard Architecture Review*, Spring 1980. Colin Rowe, in his article: "The Present Urban Predicament" in the Fall 1981 issue of *The Cornell Journal of Architecture*, distinguishes the 20th century as having the dubious distinction of making little sense of space until Pevsner's *An Outline of European Architecture*, and Giedion's *Space, Time & Architecture* appear in the early 1940's; Bernard Berenson, Geoffrey Scott and Frank LLoyd Wright being exceptions.
5. Koetter, Fred, and Rowe, Colin, *Collage City* (Massachusetts and London: The MIT Press, 1978) p. 68.
6. Schumacher, p. 86.
7. Peterson, p. 89.
8. ibid.
9. ibid.
10. Kotter, Fred, "Notes on the Inbetween," *The Harvard Architecture Review*, Spring 1980, MIT Press, p. 63.
11. Peterson, p. 89.

Fig. 16 Medieval Castle, Plan.
Fig. 17 Mies van der Rohe: Project for a 50 foot Square House, Plan, 1951.
Fig. 18 Carpaccio: St. Jerome In His Study, Oil (56¼ in. x 85½ in.) c. 1502.
Fig. 19 Mies van der Rohe: Gericke House, 1932.

HULSE PAVILION

ATLANTA, GEORGIA   1976

The HULSE PAVILION was designed as a house for a bachelor with the potential for accommodating a couple. The program called for an open living-dining area, one bedroom, a study, and service areas. It was designed in conjunction with a swimming pool, with the notion that if or when the client moved out it would be used as a guest house and a pool pavilion—as it is used today.

The structure is located in a suburban neighborhood on a narrow, deep site that slopes toward the street (south) at the front and toward the woods (north) at the rear. It is built behind an existing house that stands between the pavilion and the street. There are neighboring houses on the two contiguous sites.

The preferred view and the best orientation in terms of sunlight is to the north; there the northern wall is entirely glass. The other exposures offer less desirable vistas; those walls are essentially windowless. A high wall runs along the eastern boundary, adjacent to the house, to screen an unsightly neighbor.

The house is layered parallel to the entrance (south) facade. Upon entrance one passes through a solid and windowless wall into a dense layer that contains the service elements—the kitchen, the toilets, the storage and mechanical room. Passing through this "thickened" entry one confronts the fireplace, which may be read as a mass extracted from this dense layer. Its directional quality emphasizes the entry slot perpendicular to the front facade. A gentle curve directs passage into the living room, which, like the dining room, bedroom, and study, is open and oriented to the north and the pool—a metaphor for the natural body of water that is not there. Buried within the thick wall is a central core, which is wrapped by a stair. The stair allows one to experience the effect of the juxtaposed thickened wall in contrast to the open and interpenetrating living space.

The proportions and dimensions of the front and rear facades are identical to those of the floor plans; both are based on the ideal rectangle and its relationship to the east elevation, which is a square. Le Corbusier's system of Les Traces Regulateurs, which is used here, controls the relationship of the various elements of the facades to the whole.

20

20

21

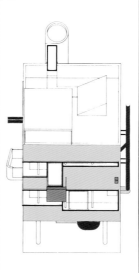

23

22, 24

Fig. 20 Peter Eisenman: House II, View of South Elevation, 1969.
Fig. 21 Richard Meier: Saltzman House, View of South Elevation, 1967.
Fig. 22 John Hejduk: Bernstein House, Projection D, 1968.
Fig. 23 Michael Graves: Hanselmann House, View of East Elevation, 1967.
Fig. 24 Charles Gwathmey: Gwathmey Residence, View of West Elevation, 1966.

HULSE PAVILION

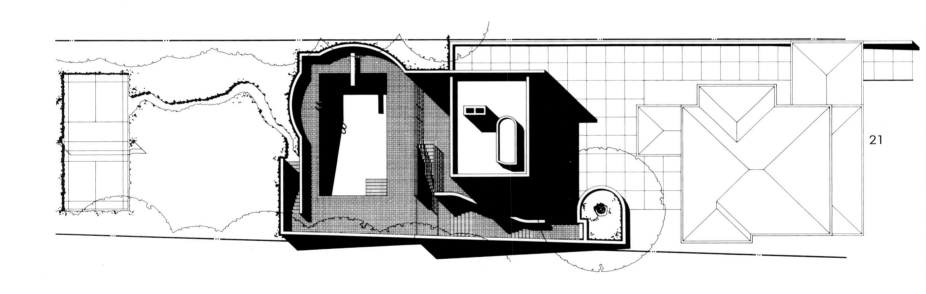

SITE PLAN

100

21

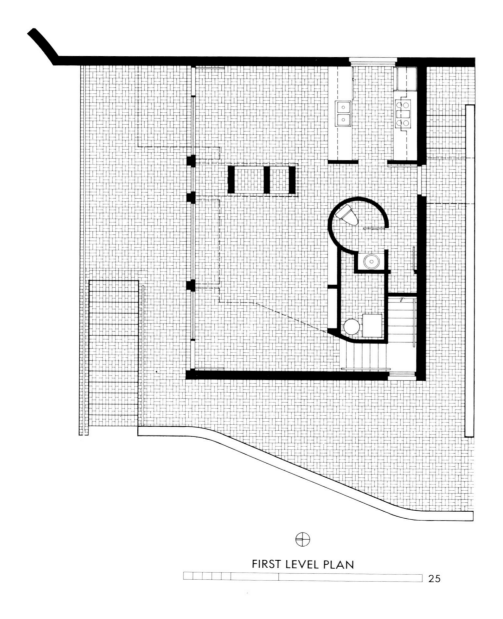

FIRST LEVEL PLAN

25

HULSE PAVILION

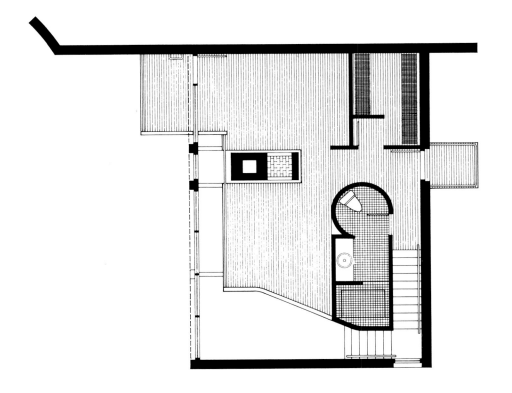

23

SECOND LEVEL PLAN

25

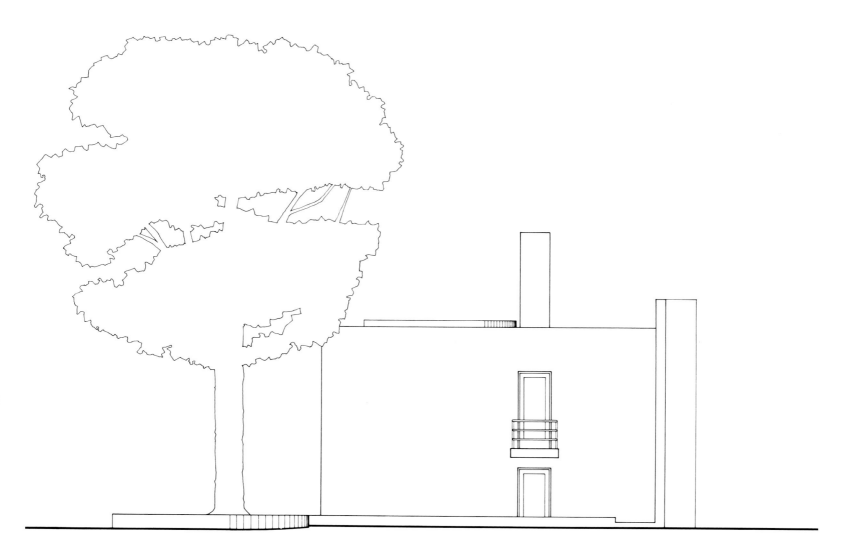

24

SOUTH ELEVATION

HULSE PAVILION

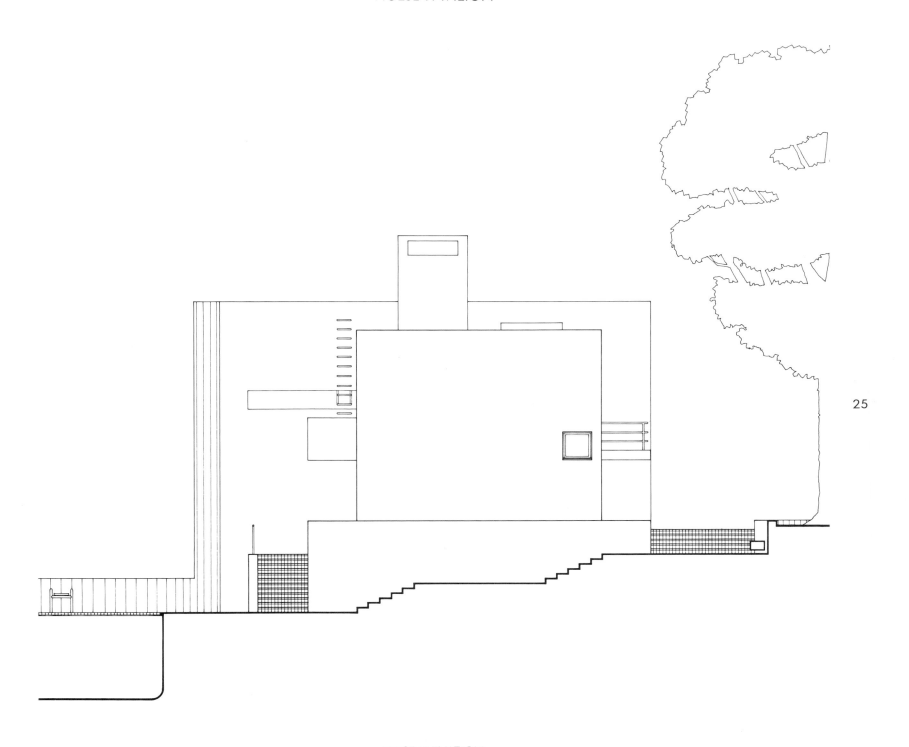

WEST ELEVATION

25

25

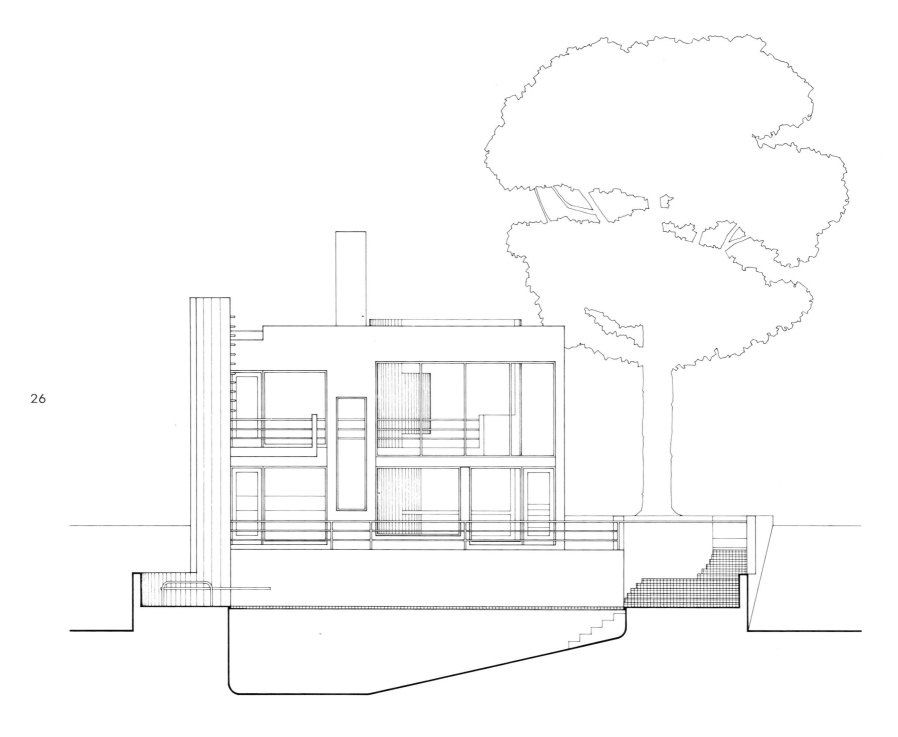

26

25

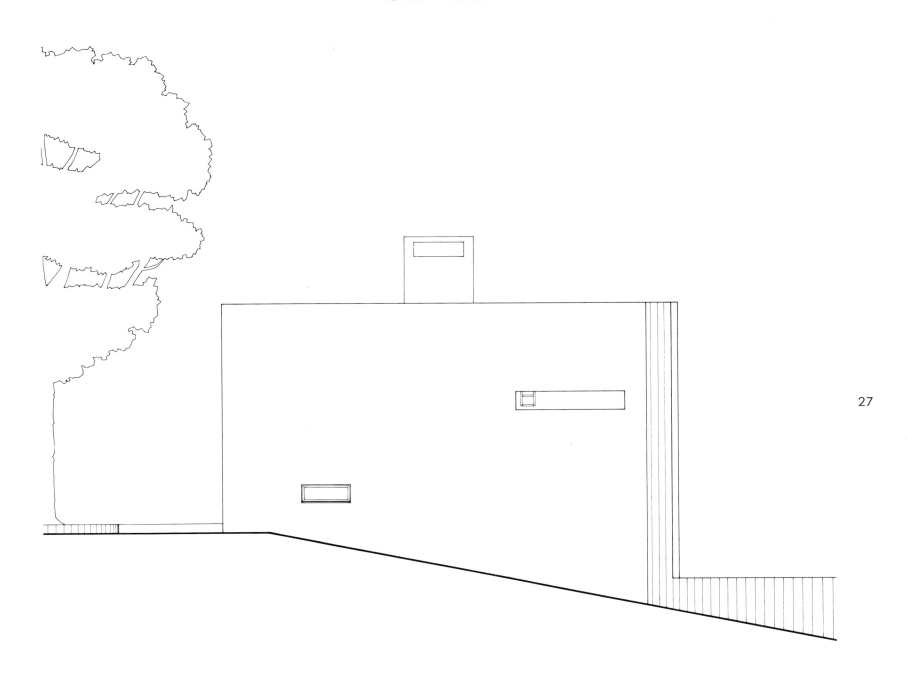

EAST ELEVATION

25

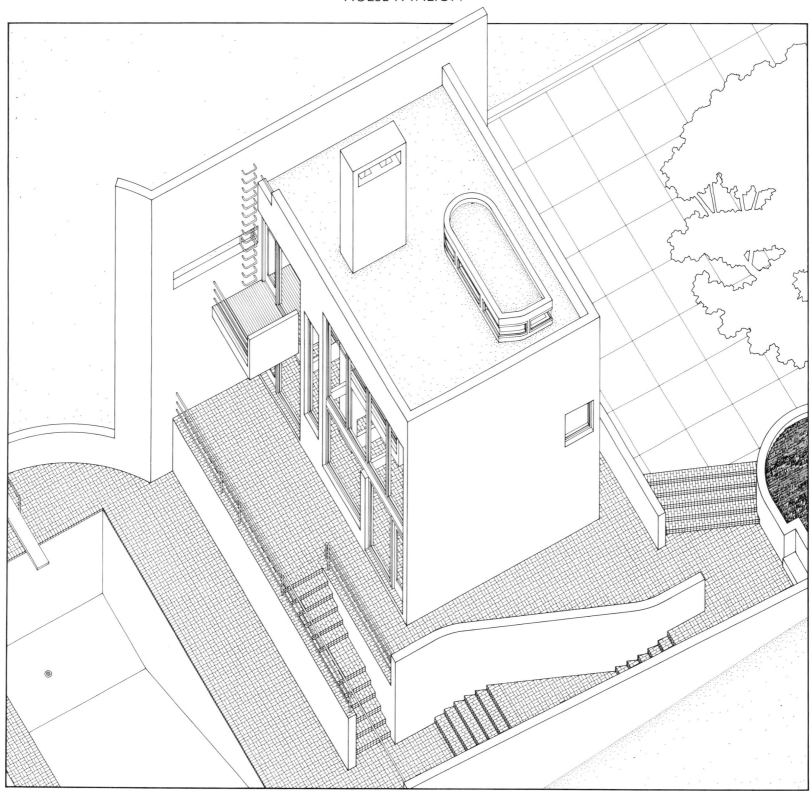

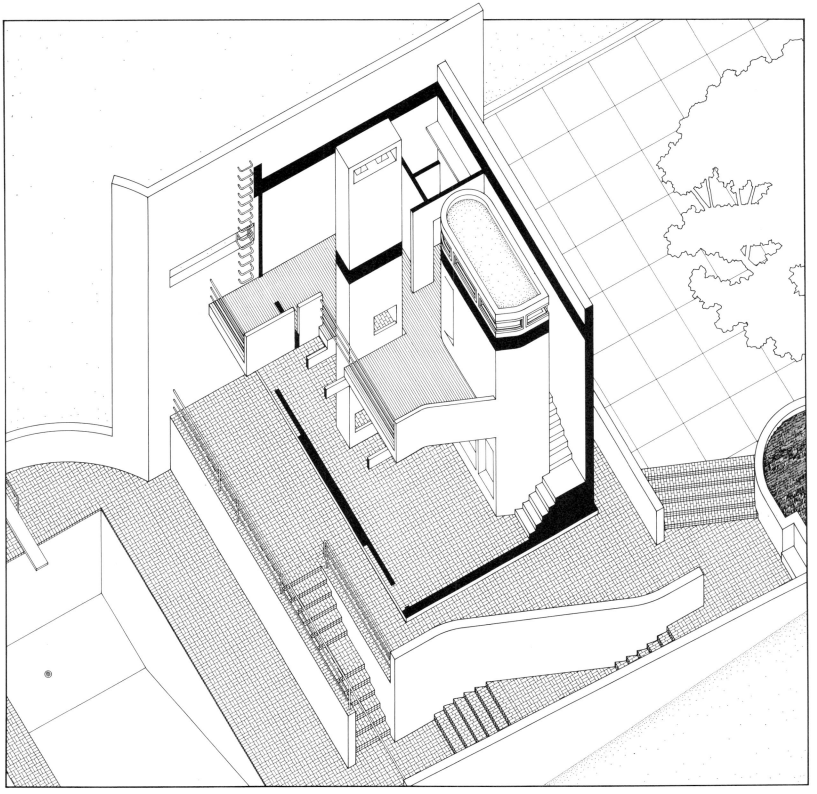

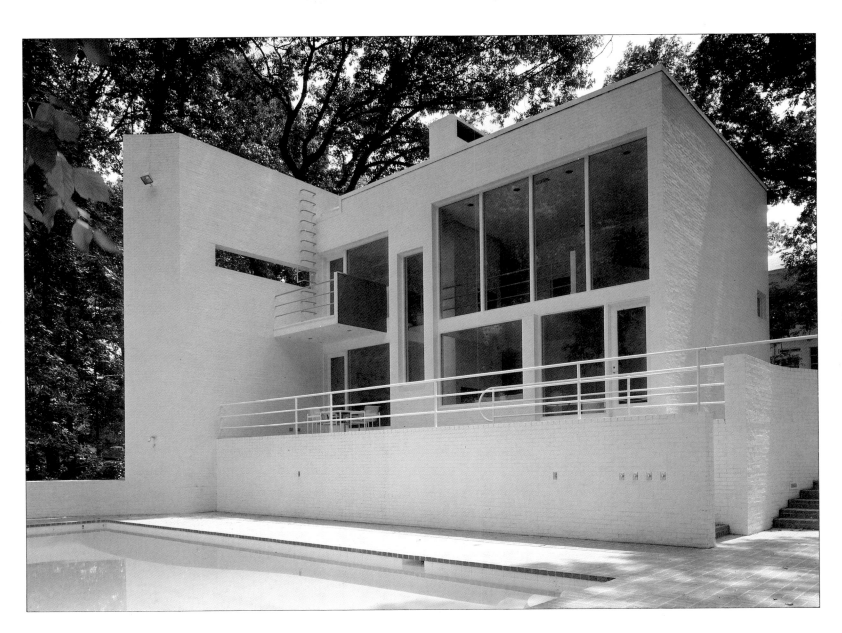

VILLA CHANG

AUGUSTA, GEORGIA   1980

The program for the VILLA CHANG called for living accommodations for a couple. He is an educator and she is a doctor of medicine. They do little formal entertaining and enjoy their library, their dogs, and their privacy, preferring an unpretentious and comfortable life style.

Located in a rural area,the site is a pie-shaped piece of property with a gentle slope perpendicular to the road that forms one of its edges. It is covered with deciduous trees and the clients wished for it to remain in this natural state. The view is down the slope toward the woods and to a lake beyond.

The impetus for the design strategy is the superimposition of two swaths that become occupied by defined solids and defined voids in the form of the main villa, out buildings, terraces, courts and garden. The most dense region of the villa occurs in the form of poche at the area of the intersection of the superimposed swaths. This dense zone contains the service elements of the program, and sponsors a clear definition of the circulation slot or corridor. The stair, also buried in the poche, is the central element and relates to both grids and both levels and is the only space that registers the angles of inflection. The poche makes it possible for the major rooms—the living room, the dining room, the bedrooms and library—to assume regular or ideal shapes.

The major organizational device is a slot that runs the length of the villa and provides access to the major spaces. Through the employment of this element a "promenade architecturale" is developed that leads the visitor from the parking court through the gate house, along a path through a box hedge and garden, and through an entry wall that helps define the entry court along this "slot." Within the house the slot offers access to the bedrooms, and the vertical circulation leads to the "piano nobile." Here the major space that contains the living and dining areas offers an elevated view of the surrounding woodland.

The elements of the plan and the facade are regulated through the use of a four-foot modular grid and a four by four (sixteen) foot module. Although this modulation is conceptual and would permit certain advantages in construction through standardization, the primary effect is a perceptual awareness of a proportional unity as one becomes cognizant of the relationships of the parts to the whole.

34

Fig. 25 Amedee Ozenfant: Still Life with a Glass of Red Wine, Oil (19⅝ in. x 24¼ in.) 1926.
Fig. 26 Palazzina Vagnuzzi, Rome, Italy, Plan, 16th C. altered by Valadier in 1810.
Fig. 27 Le Corbusier: Maison d'Artiste, Perspective Sketch, 1922.
Fig. 28 Emile Garot: apartment house, Paris, France.
Fig. 29 Le Corbusier: House for Architect's Mother, Lac LeMan,View towards Lake, 1925.
Fig. 30 Le Corbusier: House for Architect's Mother, Lac LeMan, View of Garden, 1925.

25

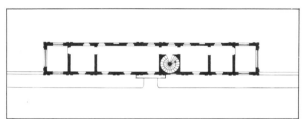
26

27

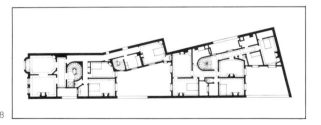
28

29, 30

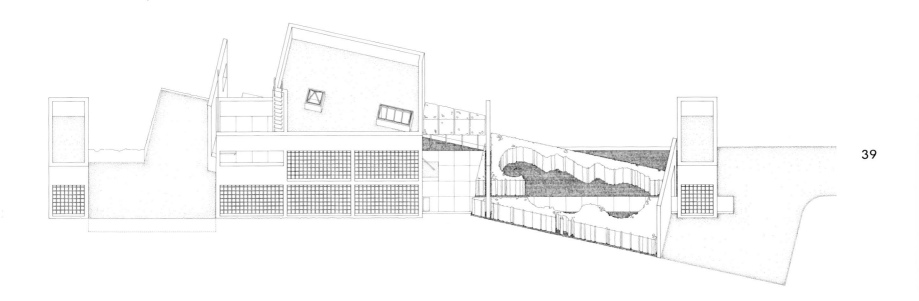

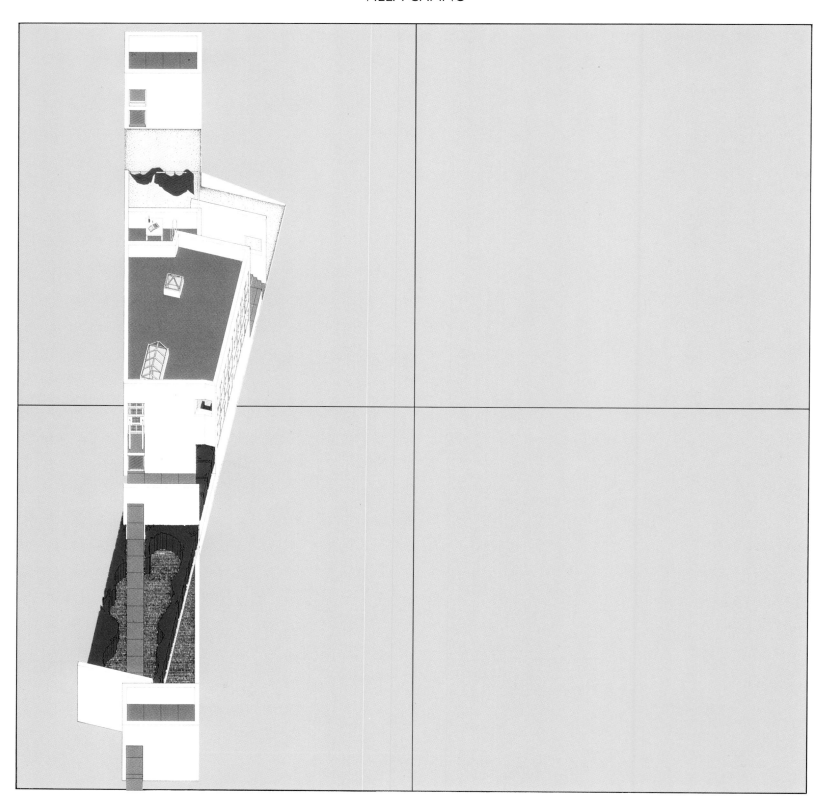

VILLA CHANG

x

43

VILLA CHANG

LAUREL, MISSISSIPPI   1981

The clients, a young couple, were interested in a residence removed from the Mississippi vernacular and similar to the HULSE PAVILION. They wished to enlarge the program, however, to include a library that could be used as another bedroom and a master bedroom with separate but equal bathrooms, and to essentially make the major spaces more generous.

The site is similar to that of the HULSE PAVILION in that it slopes toward the rear and offers a view of the landscape beyond. It is located on a residential cul-de-sac that encouraged a similar parti with closed sides and entry facade due to the proximity of the adjacent neighboring houses, and a glazed rear facade, situated on a plinth emphasizing the vista towards the rear.

As in the VILLA CHANG, a rotation or superimposition is employed to create a dynamic. In this case, two rectangles are superimposed and rotated in such a manner that the residual space created between the perimeters of each is treated as occupiable poche and contains the vertical circulation (stairs) and the service facilities. A dichotomy is established to incorporate both the characteristics of more traditional, "pre-modern" or discrete space — employing the concept of room — in the master bedroom and library and Modern space — overlapping, interpenetrating, and loosely defined — in the living/dining areas and the balcony.

As in the HULSE PAVILION, at the entry one penetrates a thickened wall; here, at an oblique angle to the facade due to the rotation of the rectangles. The facade responds to the frontal conditions of the site while the entry slot responds to the anticipated vista beyond. Upon entry one is confronted by a "built object" which frames the view and provides for associated entry needs.

The rear facade expresses the contrast between the Modern and Pre-Modern space through the juxtaposition of these two spatial types. The Pre-Modern space (expressed as mass) — in the master bedroom and the library — employs a bearing wall construction, while the Modern space (expressed as volume) — in the living/dining area — employs the free plan, piloti, and the free facade. The contiguous coexistance of these two spatial types creates a dialogue that fosters a heightened awareness and appreciation of the contrasting positive characteristics of each.

46

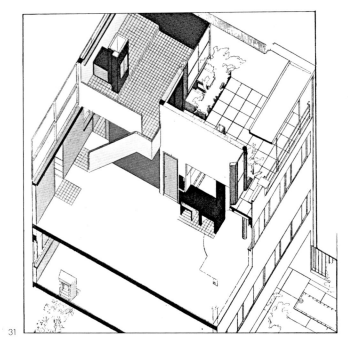
31

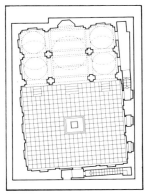
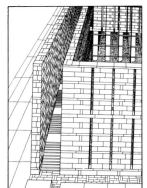
32, 33

34

Fig. 31 Le Corbusier: Maison Cook, Paris, France, Interior Axonometric, 1926.
Fig. 32 The Pearl Mosque, Red Fort, Delhi, Plan, 1638.
Fig. 33 Giuseppe Terragni: Danteum, Rome, Italy, Perspective, 1938.
Fig. 34 La Villa Gamberaia, Settignano, Italy, View below plinth, c. 1610.

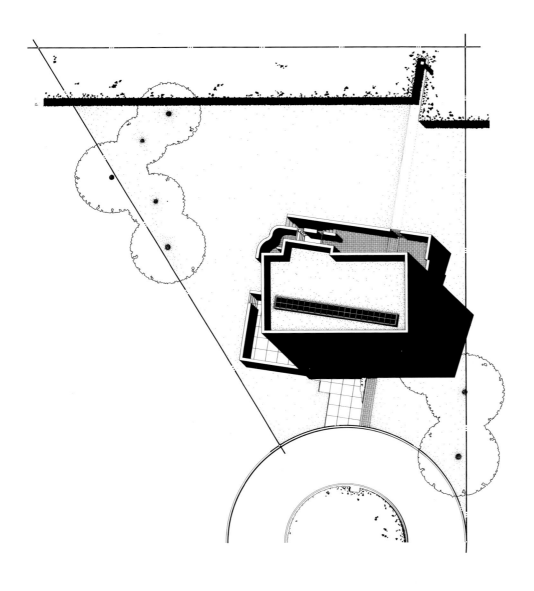

SITE PLAN

100

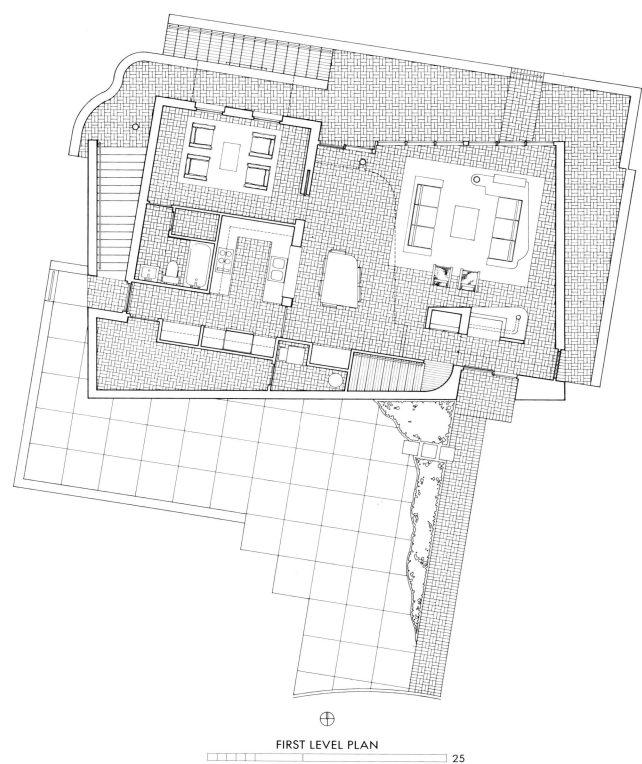

48

FIRST LEVEL PLAN

25

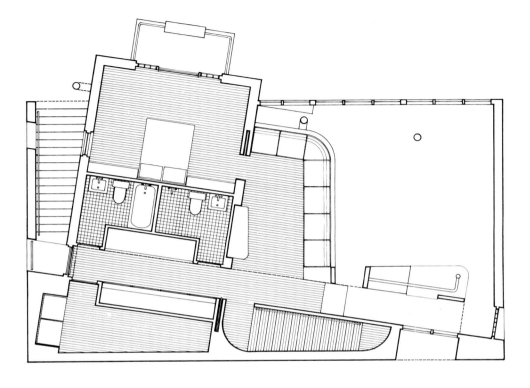

49

SECOND LEVEL PLAN

25

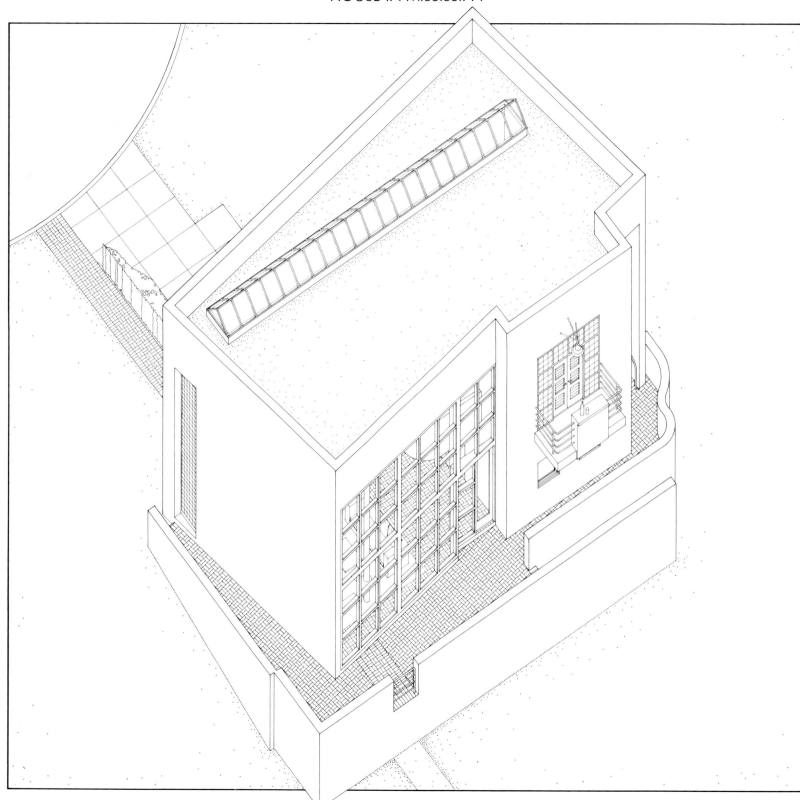

50

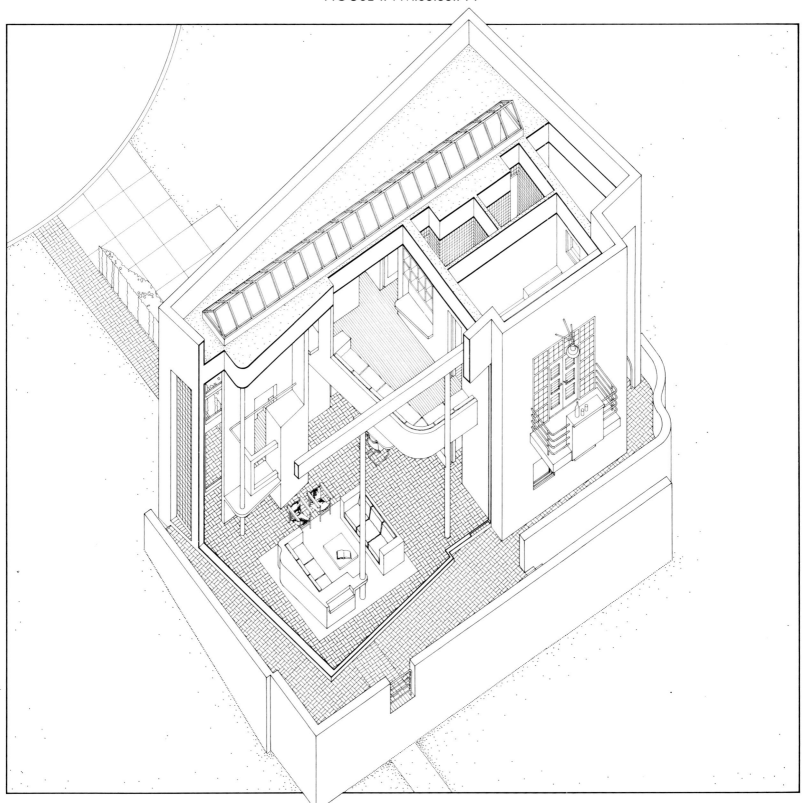

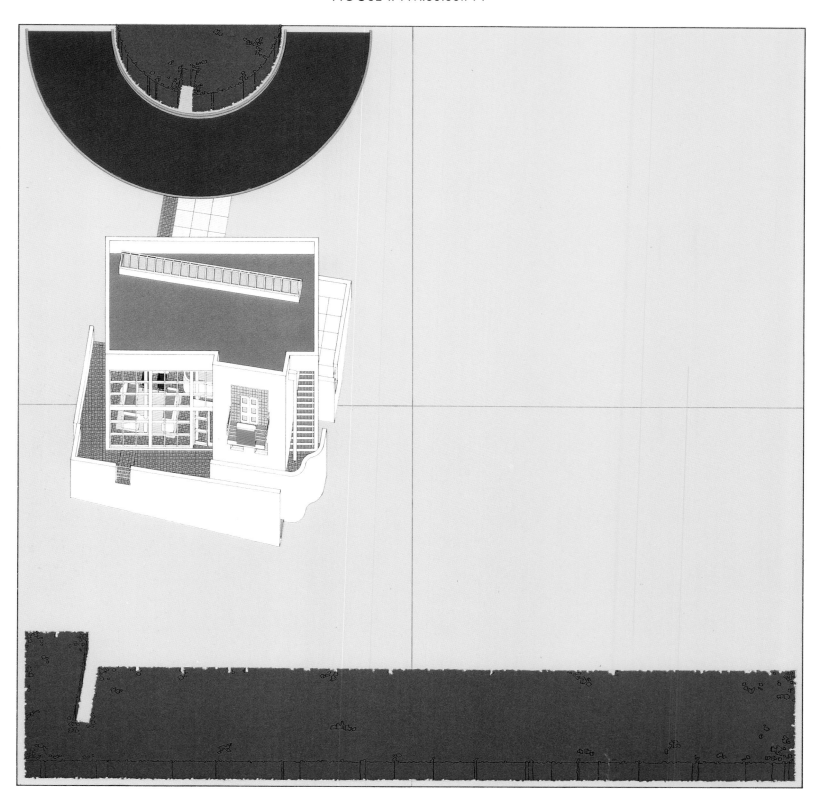

52

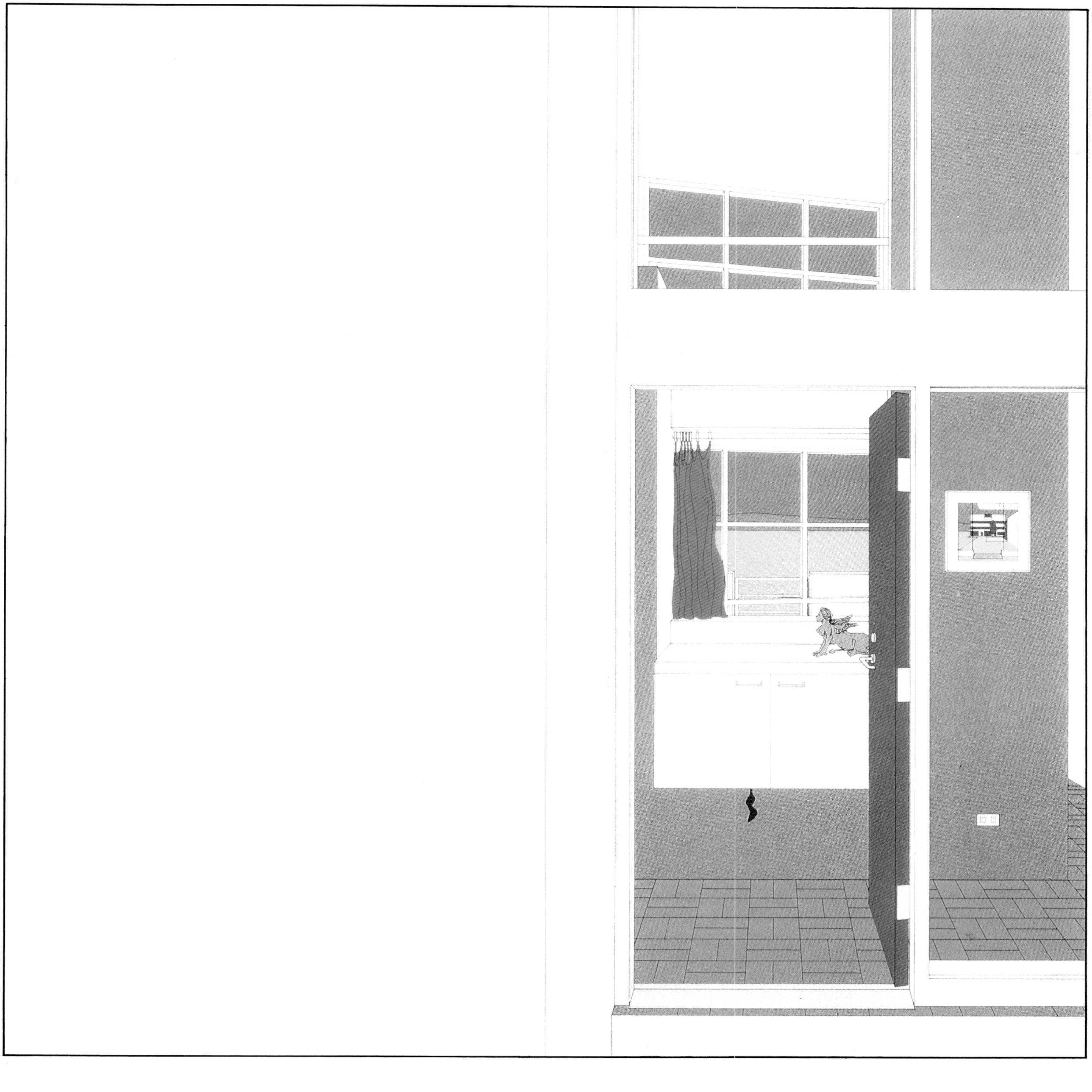

54

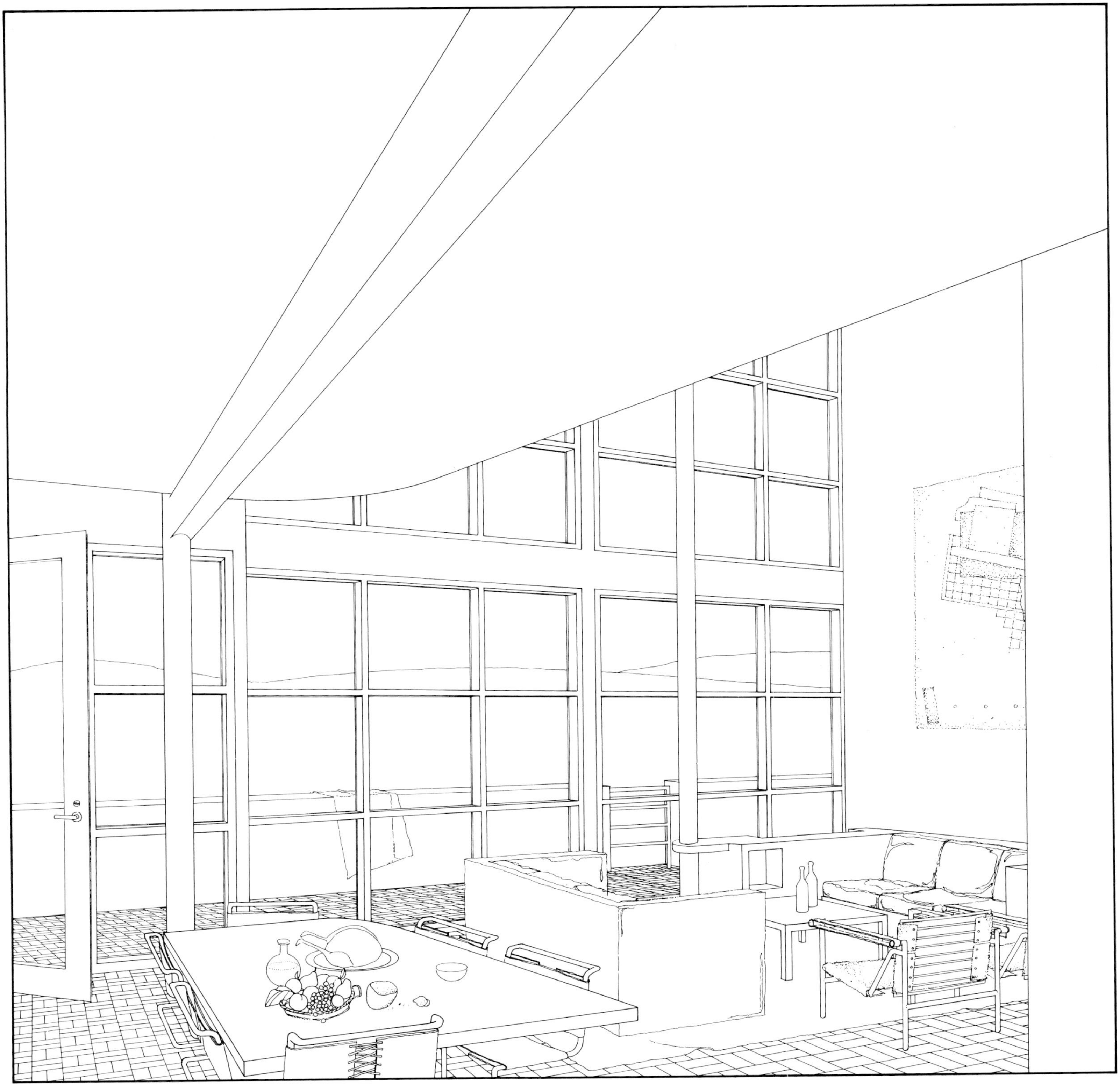

SON OF CHANG

AUGUSTA, GEORGIA   1982

The program for the SON OF CHANG was essentially identical to that for the VILLA CHANG; however, due to the architectural responses dictated by the site conditions, the ultimate form of the house is quite different.

The site is located in a suburban rather than a rural situation, so it was necessary to control the vistas and to screen the adjacent neighbors. The site is restricted as only a portion, defined by the road and a narrow fissure that divides the site in half, is buildable. Located on an edge of this buildable portion, the house creates a barrier between a defined grassy area and the adjacent property. This area and a slot-like space with a controlled vista adjacent to the house are defined by the precise, clipped edge of the topiary. A curvilinear path is carved through this dense vegetation leading to the wooded area on the other side of the fissure that is left in its natural state.

The main organizational element of the house is a tapering hallway along which the major, locally symmetrical rooms are organized—similar to the VILLA CHANG. The main block of the house, the man-made structure ("order"), has a bent appendage that externally registers a response to the natural conditions ("chaos") of the site. This rotation of the library block also identifies this unit as having a different and special quality and function removing it spiritually and physically from the orthogonal and the functionally related activities of the central block of the house.

At the point of rotation, poche is employed to effectively resolve the transition from the entry hall into the library. A tight, restrictive, curvilinear entry hall is "carved" from the poche in order to emphasize the contrast between the passive, closed and internally oriented condition of the library and the more active, open nature of the other rooms. The rotation of the library element is acknowledged and registered in plan, elevation, and in three dimensions in other areas of the house. These traces or clues inform and reward the careful observer.

An attempt is made to reveal the character of the rooms behind the main (garden) facade through their fenestration treatment—size, shape, location—as they face the regularized green space from which they will be revealed. A system of regulating lines is employed to organize these windows in the facade.

58

35

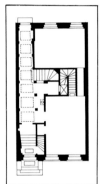 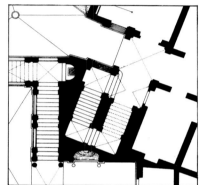

36, 37

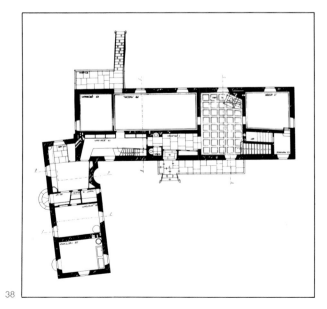

38

Fig. 35 The Theatre at La Palazzina (Villa Gori), Siena, Italy, 17th C.
Fig. 36 Erik Lallerstedt: Architect's Own House, Stockholm, Sweden, Plan, 1923.
Fig. 37 Palazzo Maccarani, Rome, Italy, Plan.
Fig. 38 Erik Gunnar Asplund: Villa Snellman, First Scheme, Djursholm, Sweden, Plan, 1917-18.

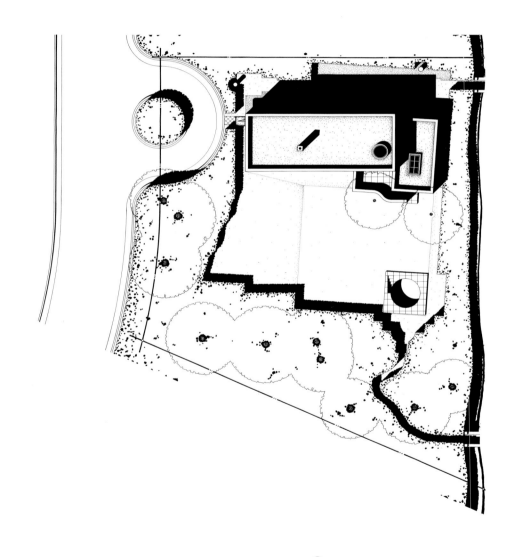

SITE PLAN

100

60

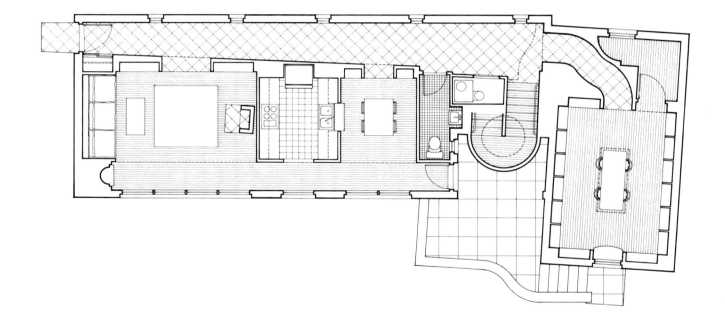

FIRST LEVEL PLAN

25

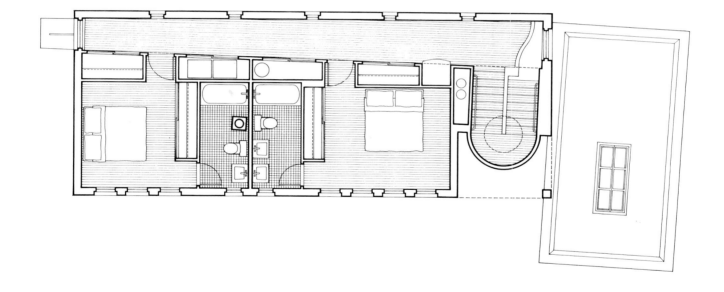

SECOND LEVEL PLAN

25

62

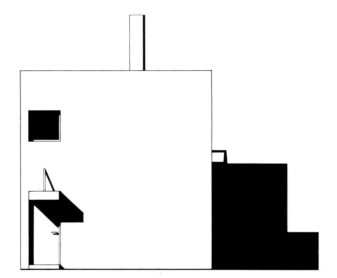

WEST ELEVATION

25

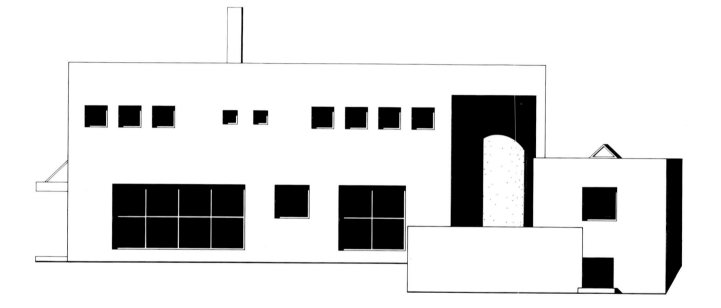

SOUTH ELEVATION

25

64

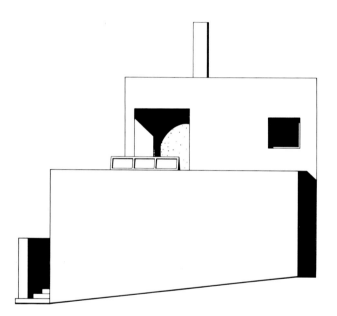

EAST ELEVATION

25

SON OF CHANG

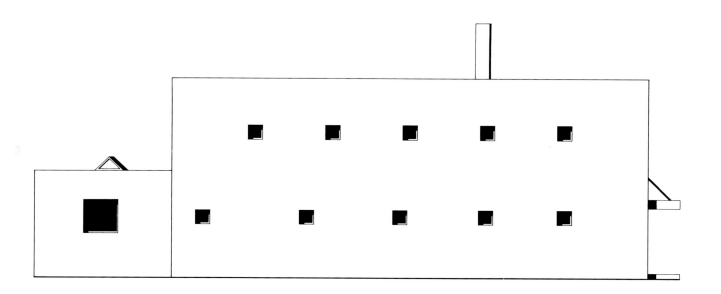

65

NORTH ELEVATION

25

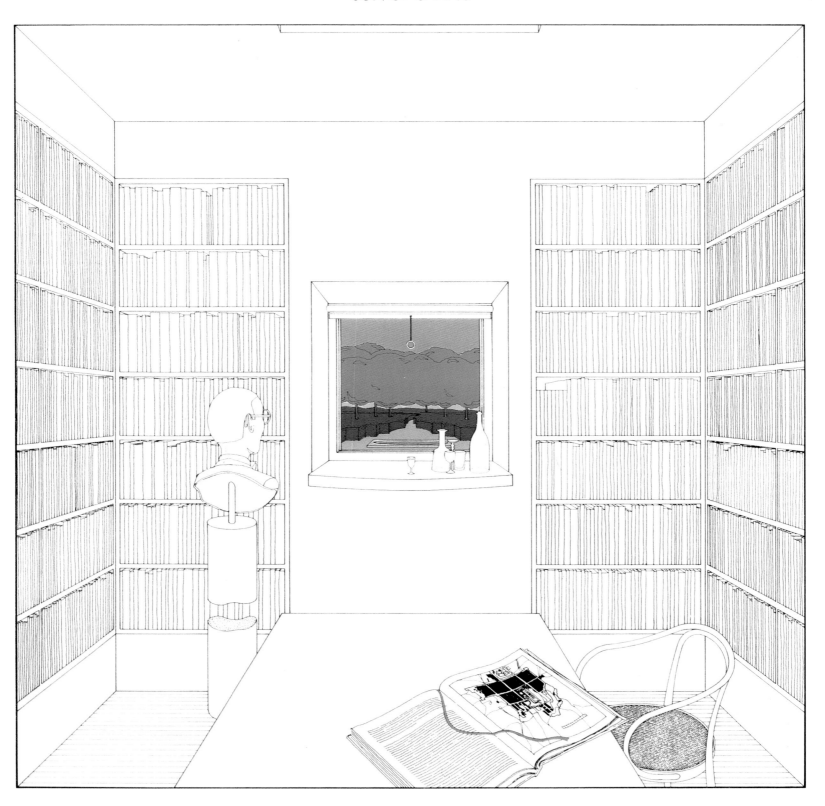

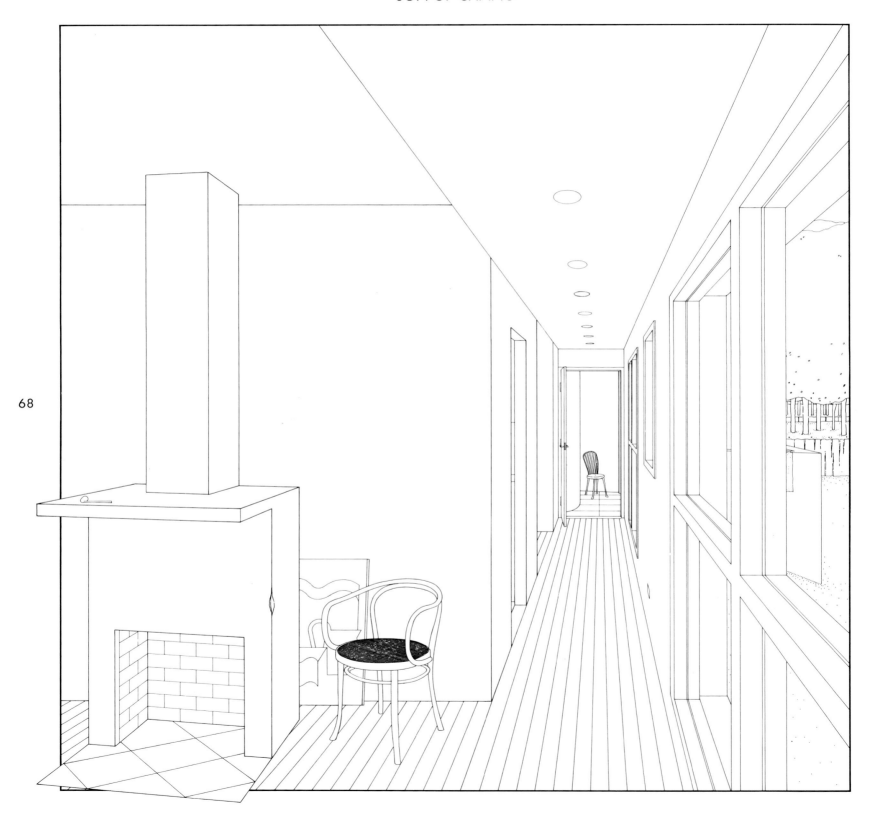

68

70

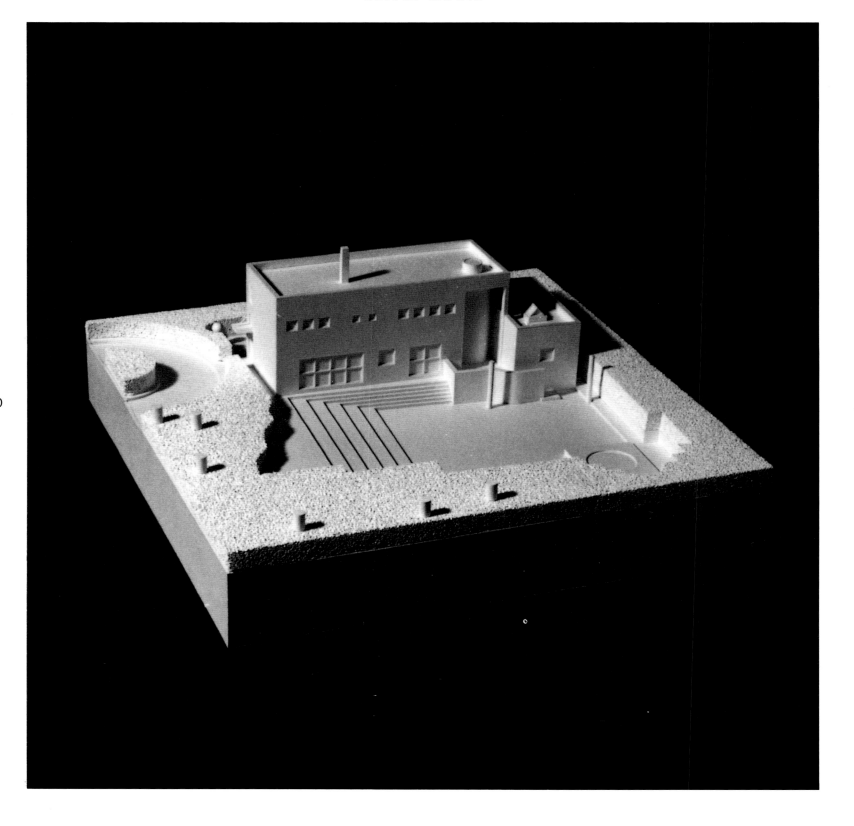

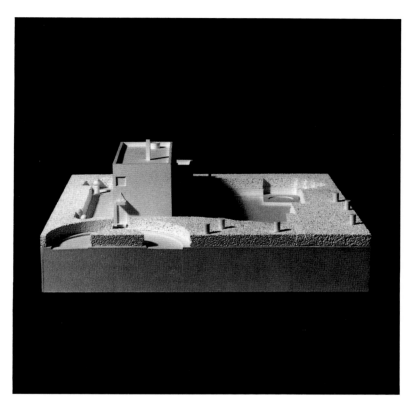
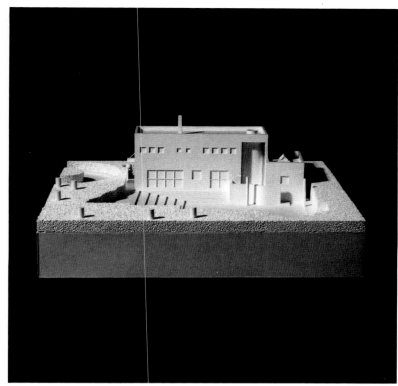
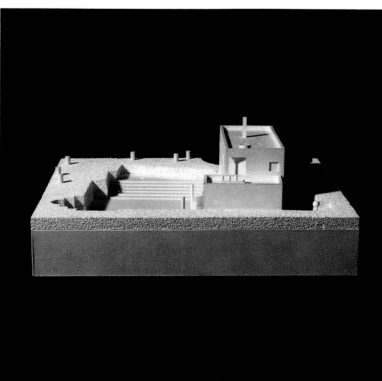
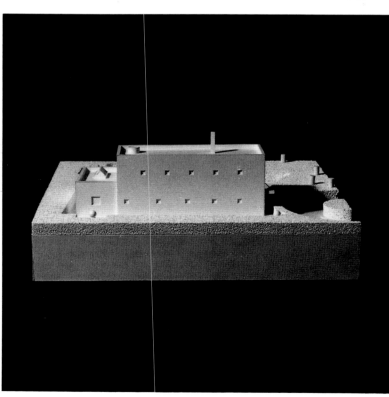

GARDEN PAVILION

ATLANTA, GEORGIA   1985

The client's need for a physical and mental retreat from the numerous distractions of a busy household and a need for the remote accommodation of guests led to the creation of this study/guest pavilion as an ancillary structure behind the existing house. The program called for a large studio space and service facilities.

The structure is rotated off the established grid of the residence and then elevated on pilotis (creating a sheltered car park) to dissociate it from its surroundings. The two major facades are then treated differently: a rather closed public courtyard facade, with a basketball hoop to engage the weary scholar, and a translucent wall, facing into the garden.

The pavilion hovers on the edge of an Italianate Renaissance box garden which reestablishes the orthogonal system of the other elements on the site; however, a swath is cut through this order that marks the center of the pavilion and registers its presence. These two axes—that of the garden and that of the center of the pavilion—come together at a totem, the focal point of the garden.

Within this spare and relatively unrevealing box is a private domain which refers to the larger residence through the orientation of its dense core. The tightly compacted form of the poche that borders the ideal space on three sides and this dense free-standing core accommodate the functional necessities of the program. The core contains the bathroom, the kitchen, the mechanical room, book storage, a closet, and loft space for sleeping and storage above. The poche element contains a couch, a work desk, book shelves, vertical print storage and a stair, carved into the dense poche that leads to a sleeping loft nestled in the cloud above.

The core can be read both as an object isolated by its figural qualities on an open plane and as poche creating and serving as an edge for the negative space from which it has been removed. References to certain aspects of urban planning, Pre-Modern/Modern space are employed and a spatial dynamic is created through the use of rotation and superimposition. A sense of movement results in the ancillary spaces that helps to heighten the sense of repose that exists in the major space through contrast and juxtoposition.

72

39

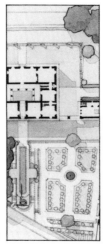 

40, 41

42, 43

Fig. 39 Le Corbusier: La loge a Villa Savoye, Poissy, France, View of East Elevation, 1929-31.
Fig. 40 La Villa Gamberaia, Settignano, Italy, Detail of Garden Plan, c. 1610.
Fig. 41 Antonello da Messina: S. Jerome in his Study, Oil on limewood (45.7 cm x 36.2 cm) c. 1456.
Fig. 42 Pierre Chareau: Maison de Verre, Paris, France, View of glass wall from kitchen, 1928-32.
Fig. 43 Thomas Jefferson: Monticello, Albemarle County, Virginia, View of alcove bed, 1771.

GARDEN PAVILION

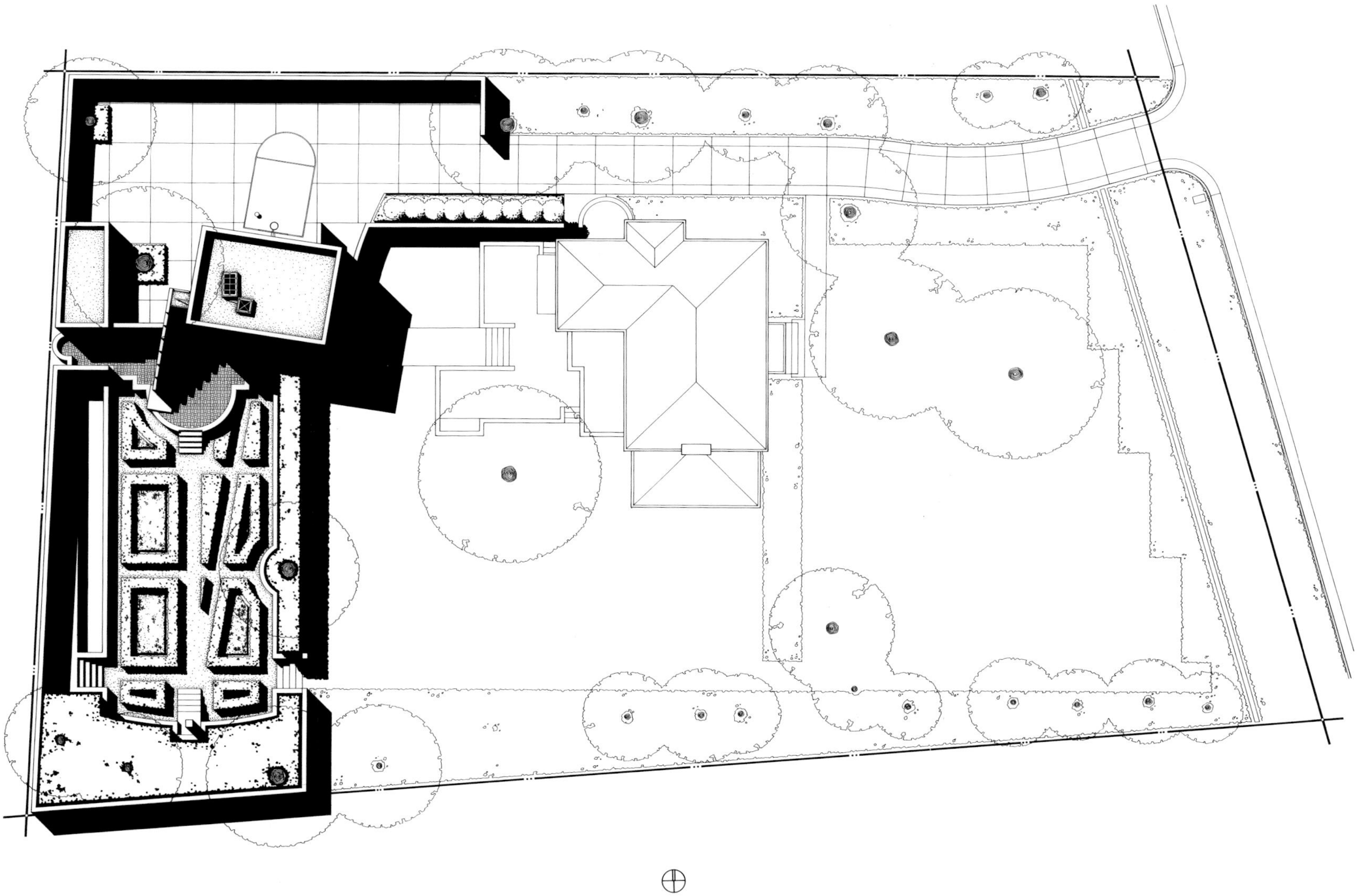

73

SITE PLAN

100

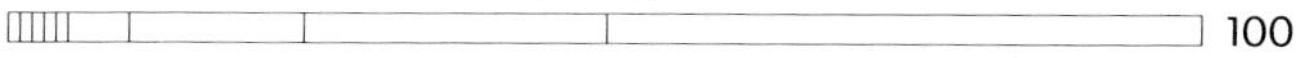

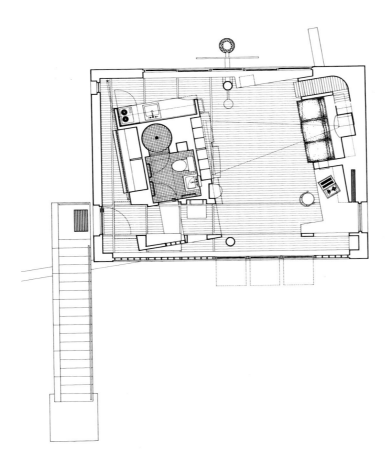

FLOOR PLAN

GARDEN PAVILION

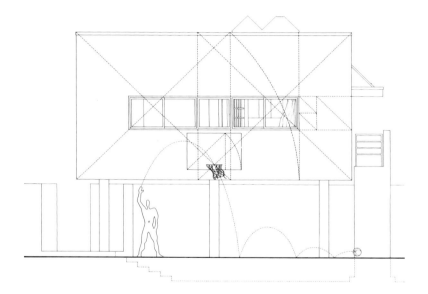

NORTH ELEVATION

25

GARDEN PAVILION

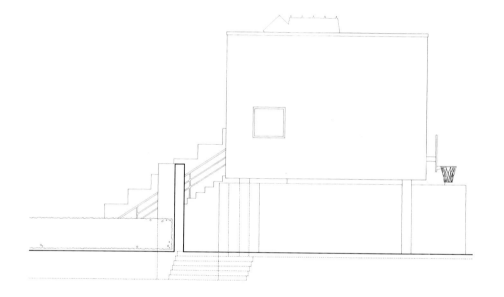

EAST ELEVATION

25

GARDEN PAVILION

78

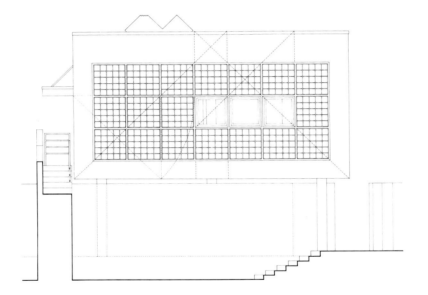

SOUTH ELEVATION

25

GARDEN PAVILION

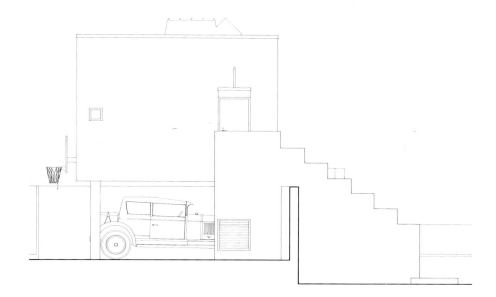

WEST ELEVATION

25

GARDEN PAVILION

80

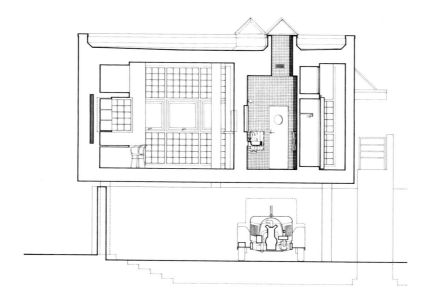

LONGITUDINAL SECTION

25

GARDEN PAVILION

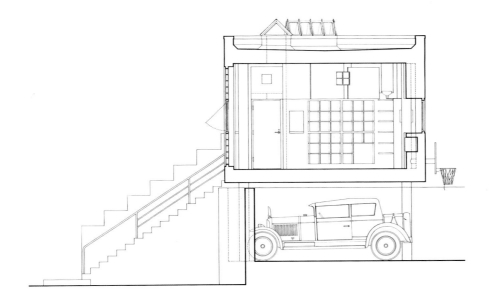

81

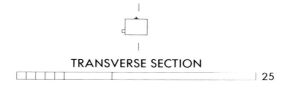

TRANSVERSE SECTION

25

82

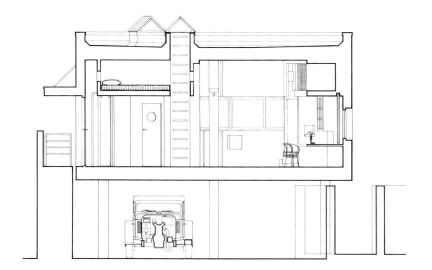

LONGITUDINAL SECTION

25

GARDEN PAVILION

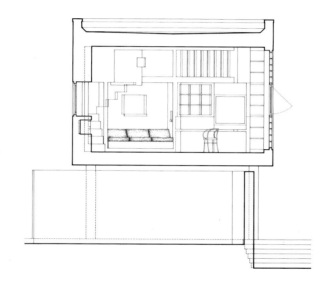

83

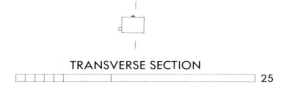

TRANSVERSE SECTION

25

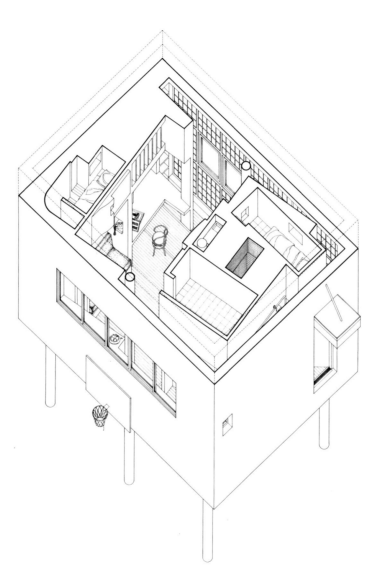

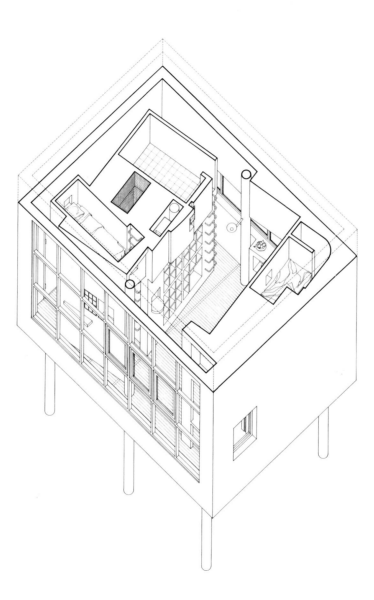

90

94

HULSE RESIDENCE

The clients were newly married and without additional family. They lived in a pavilion that I designed for the husband when he was a bachelor located on the same site (See p. 20). They wished to build a villa on the same site adjacent to the pavilion. An existing house that was located between the pavilion and the street was demolished to accommodate the new structure.

Certain references to the existing site conditions inform the design of the villa. The side walls of the pavilion are extended to form what might be perceived as an abstract modern frame or grid within which a more traditional Pre-Modern structure is constructed. This structure is slightly rotated to aline with an oblique edge of the site that is defined by an existing wall, thereby dramatizing the relationship of the Pre-Modern and the Modern structures. Since the site slopes dramatically to the street and the extention of the pavilion walls results in a rather narrow building, the villa has four stories. The private entry is at the lower level through the garage and the public entry is at the second level, up a tapering exterior stair that places the visitor on the transverse axis of the rotated villa.

The front facade faces the major view toward a wooded park across the street. The most important spaces—the double height living room and the bedroom, therefore, are oriented in this direction and registered on this elevation. The animated, garden elevation reveals the activities that occur behind it, in contrast to the east elevation, which simply forms a screen wall that reinforces an edge of the site. The service court facade is essentially a "section cut," creating a defining edge for the service court.

The rotated volume of the Pre-Modern structure is punctured by a slot, parallel to the extended walls of the pavilion, that originates within the existing pavilion. Occurring on all levels this slot serves as a circulation corridor along which the rooms of the villa are organized. All the major rooms are idealized and locally symmetrical; however, in the living area a more modern interpretation of space is manifest in its double height, interpenetrating, loosely defined treatment. It is important, however, that the major rooms evoke a sense of repose and that the effects of rotation and superimposition be experienced to the largest extent in the active spaces —the slot, the stair entries, the main entry, and in the space that mediates between the rotated structures and the extended walls— the occupiable poche.

100

Fig. 44 Giuseppe Terragni: La Casa del Fascio, Como, Italy, West Elevation, 1932-36.
Fig. 45 Raphael: Palazzo Pandolfini, Florence, Italy, Detail of Plan, 1520-29.
Fig. 46 Carpaccio: La Nascita della Vergine, Oil (126 cm x 129 cm) 1504-08.
Fig. 47 Villa Capponi, Arcetri, Italy, View of parterre garden, c. 1572.
Fig. 48 Rob. Mallet-Stevens: La Villa de Noailles, Hyeres, France, 1924-33.

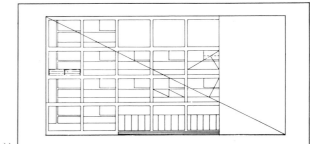

44

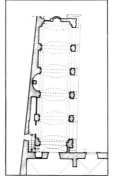

45, 46

47

48

HULSE RESIDENCE

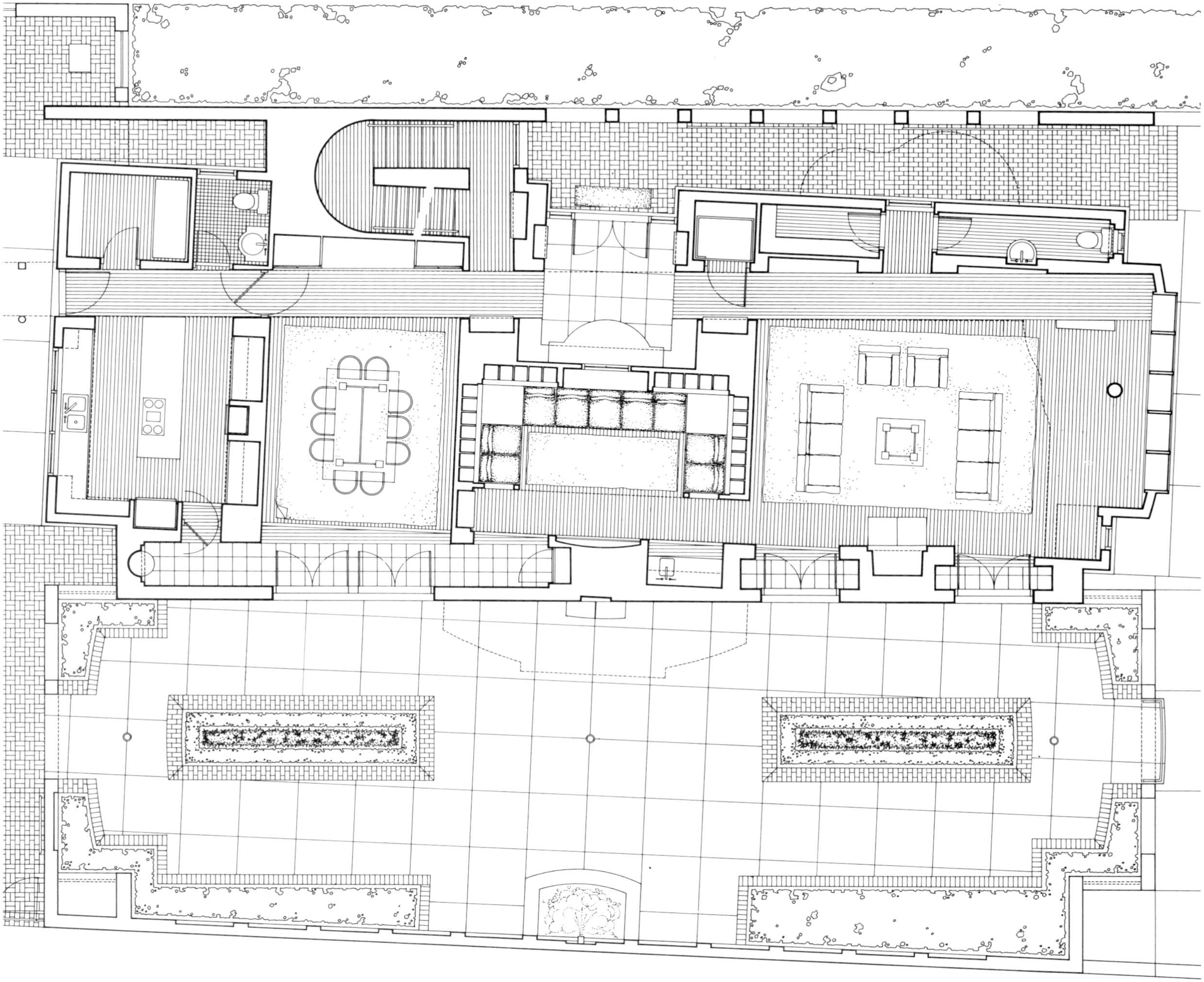

103

FIRST LEVEL PLAN

25

HULSE RESIDENCE

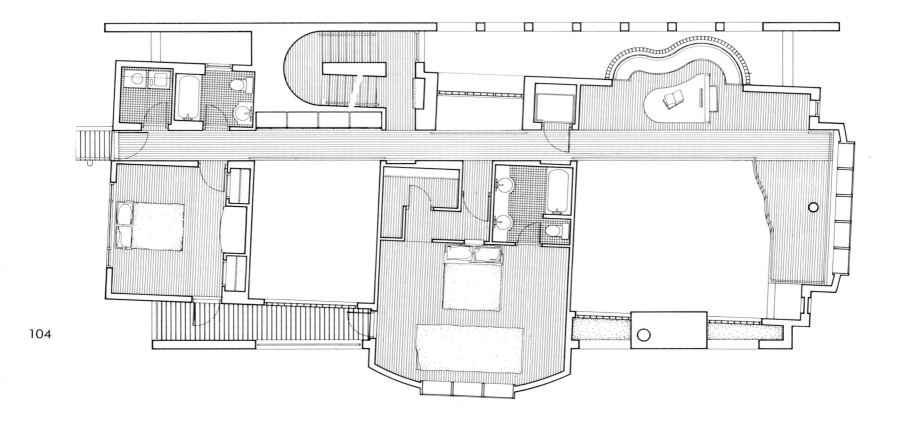

104

$\oplus$

SECOND LEVEL PLAN

25

HULSE RESIDENCE

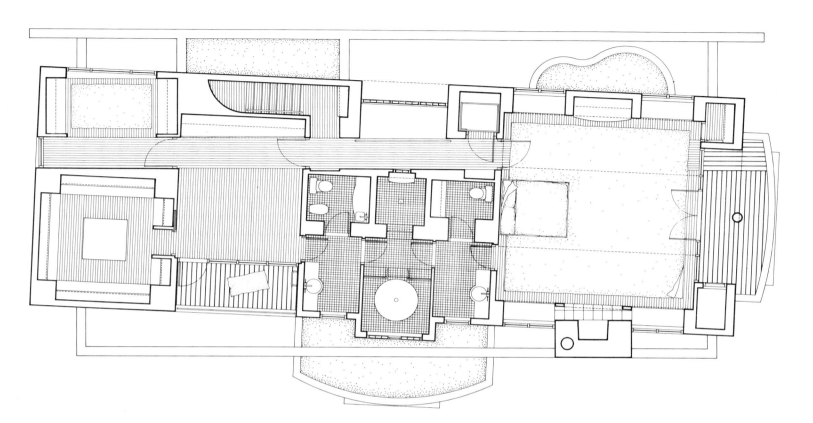

105

25

HULSE RESIDENCE

SOUTH ELEVATION

25

HULSE RESIDENCE

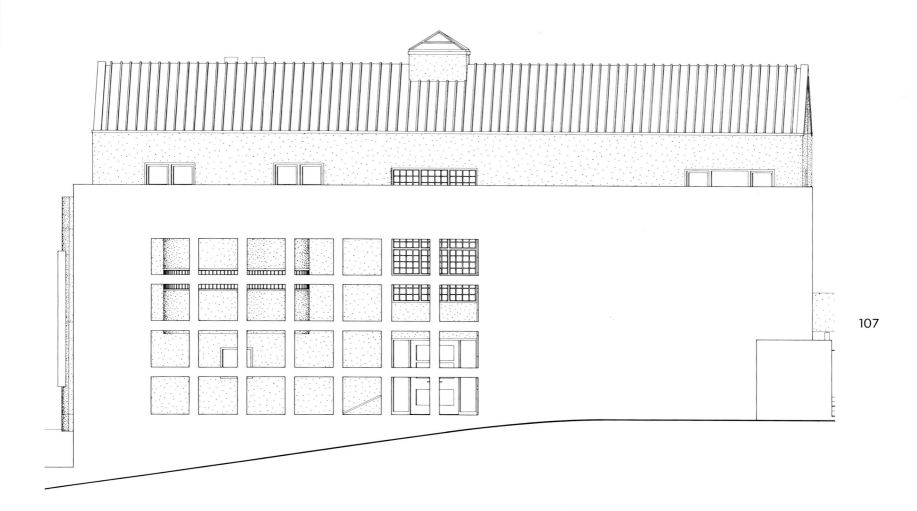

107

EAST ELEVATION

25

HULSE RESIDENCE

108

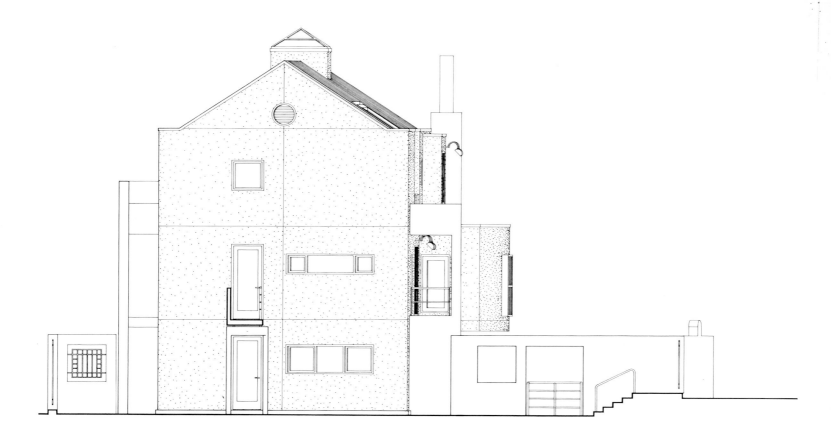

NORTH ELEVATION

25

HULSE RESIDENCE

109

WEST ELEVATION

25

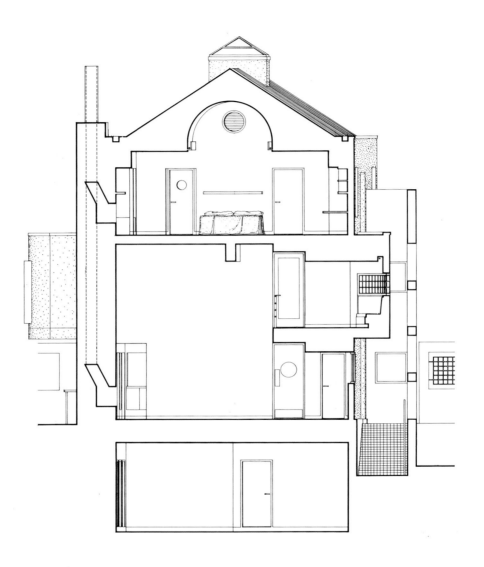

TRANSVERSE SECTION

25

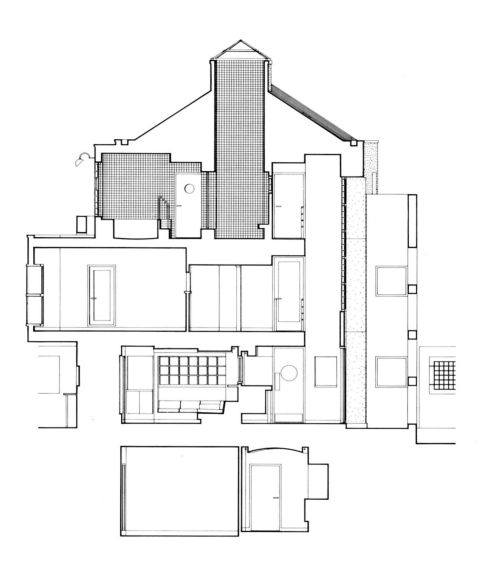

TRANSVERSE SECTION

⊢───────────────────┤ 25

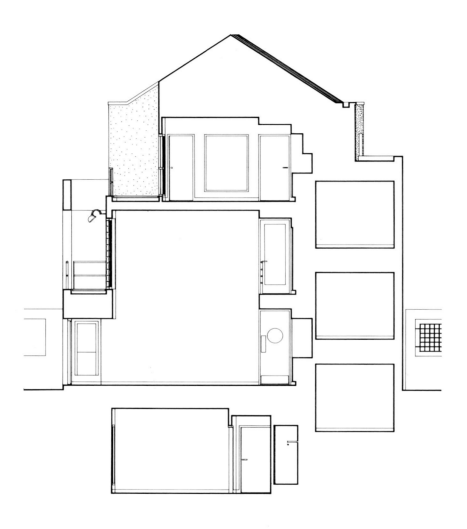

TRANSVERSE SECTION

25

TRANSVERSE SECTION

25

122

HULSE RESIDENCE

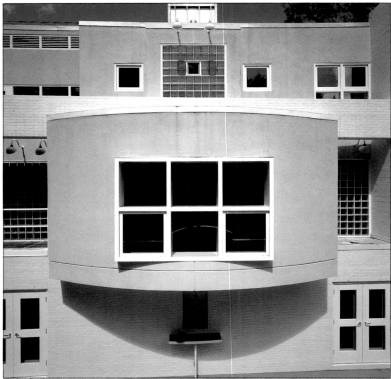

126

In 1972 Wittenborn & Company published a thin, white covered book entitled *Five Architects*. The book originally intended to document the work presented at a meeting of architects, who were friends, held at the Museum of Modern Art in 1969. Since it took three years to compile the work discussed and exhibited, additional work was included by each of the five architects. It was a book about architecture—for architects—and resulted in a great deal of discussion (both pro and con) by those interested in the art of architecture.

Tony Ames was a student when this book was first seen by the literate architectural audience. It has obviously had an important influence on his career as an architect. The early works presented here, *FIVE HOUSES*, show the intensity of care and the passion that he possesses for the thinking, the drawing, and the making of architecture which is on one hand modest and on the other heroic.

Richard Meier
New York
1987

ACKNOWLEDGEMENTS

To those in the profession—both in practice and academia—who through example and encouragement made the projects in this book possible. To Kevin Lippert who made the book possible. To Ellen Soroka who read the text and made valuable suggestions and contributions. To Alan Brown who arrived at the right time and saw the project through and to my family who lent me the time—something I can never repay.

The following people worked in my office and assisted with the projects in this book:

Alan Brown
Isa Caballero
Martine Cornier
Susan Desko
John Fisher
William Marquand
Margaret Minor
William Pantsari
Kelin Perry
Bailey Pope
Gilbert Rampy
Ellen Soroka
J. James Strange
Clark Tefft

CREDITS

ILLUSTRATION CREDITS

Fig. 1 Anthony Ames, 1985.
Fig. 2 J.-F. Blondel, *Architecture Francoise* (Paris, 1754) p. 236.
Fig. 3 Bruno Zevi, *Omaggio a Terragni* (Milano: Etas/Kompass, 1968) p. 92.
Fig. 4 Anthony Ames, 1982.
Fig. 5 Val Warke.
Fig. 6 Paul Letarouilly, *VATICAN I, II, III* (Paris: A. Morel, 1882) pl. 115.
Fig. 7 Giovanni Battista Nolli, *La Nuova Topografia di Roma*, 1748.
Fig. 8 Le Corbusier, *Oeuvre Complete 1910-1929* (Zurich: Les Editions D'Architecture, 1964) p. 111
       [Redrawn by Stuart Cohen and Steven Hurtt].
Fig. 9 After Colin Rowe, "The Present Urban Predicament," *The Cornell Journal of Architecture*
       (Ithaca: Cornell University: Department of Architecture, 1981) p. 28.
Fig. 10 Ibid.
Fig. 11 Peter Murry, *Renaissance Architecture* (New York: Abrams, 1971) p. 181.
Fig. 12 Philip Johnson, *Mies van der Rohe* (New York: The Museum of Modern Art, 1947) p. 88.
Fig. 13 Paul Letarouilly, *Edifices de Rome Moderne* (Paris: A. Morel, 1874).
Fig. 14 No. 13 Lincoln's Inn Fields, *A Gorden Fraser Card*, The Trustees of Sir John Soane's Museum.
Fig. 15 Dorothy Stroud, *Sir John Soane,* Architect (London: Faber and Faber, 1984) p. 91.
Fig. 16 MacGibbon and Ross, *The Castellated and Domestic Architecture of Scotland* (Edinburg,
       1982) p. 311 [Redrawn by Clark Tefft].
Fig. 17 Johnson, p. 180.
Fig. 18 Carpaccio, ST. JEROME IN HIS STUDY, Scuola Degli Schiavoni (Venice c. 1502).
Fig. 19 Wolf Tegethoff, *Mies van der Rohe: Die Villen und Landhausprojekte* (Bonn: Kaiser Wilhelm
       Museum der Stadt Krefeld, 1981) p. 15.14.
Fig. 20 *Five Architects: Eisenman, Graves, Gwathmey, Hejduk, Meier* (New York: Oxford University
       Press, 1972) p. 37.
Fig. 21 Ibid, p. 129.
Fig. 22 Ibid, p. 101.
Fig. 23 Ibid, p. 52.
Fig. 24 Ibid, p. 69.
Fig. 25 Amedee Ozenfant, STILL LIFE WITH A GLASS OF RED WINE, Offentliche Kunstsammlung
       (Basel, 1921).
Fig. 26 I. Belli Barsali, *Ville di Roma* (Milano: Edizioni Sisar, 1970) p. 449.
Fig. 27 Le Corbusier,p. 53.
Fig. 28 Michael Dennis, *Court & Garden* (Cambridge: MIT Press, 1986) p. 219 [Redrawn by
       Clark Tefft].
Fig. 29 Le Corbusier, p. 74.
Fig. 30 Ibid, p. 75.
Fig. 31 L'Arch. Vivante, IX (Fall and Winter 1927).
Fig. 32 Henri Stierlin, *Encyclopaedia of World Architecture* (London: Macmillan Press, 1977) p. 408.
Fig. 33 Thomas L. Schumacher, *Il Danteum di Terragni* (Roma: Officina Edizioni, 1980) p. 48. English
       Edition, The Danteum (Princeton: Princeton Architectural Press, 1985).
Fig. 34 Giuseppe Zocchi, *Vedute di Firenze e Della Toscana* (Firenze: Libreria Editrice Fiorentina,
       1981) p. 177.
Fig. 35 Edith Wharton, *Italian Villas and their Gardens* (New York: The Century Co., 1904) p. 73
       [Painting by Maxfield Parrish].
Fig. 36 Stuart Knight, "Swedish Grace: Modern Classicism in Stockholm," *International Architect*
       (Number 8: Volume 1, 1982) p. 37 [Redrawn by Clark Tefft].
Fig. 37 Paul Letarouilly, *Edifices de Rome Moderne* (Paris: A. Morel, 1874).
Fig. 38 Stuart Wrede, *The Architecture of Erik Gunnar Asplund* (Cambridge: MIT Press, 1980) p. 52.
Fig. 39 Le Corbusier, *Oeuvre Complete 1929-1934* (Zurich: Les Editions D'Architecture, 1964) p. 28.
Fig. 40 J.C. Shepherd and G.A. Jellicoe, *Italian Gardens of the Renaissance* (London: Ernest Benn
       Ltd., 1925) pl. 50.
Fig. 41 Antonello da Messina, ST. JEROME IN HIS STUDY, The National Gallery (London, c. 1456).
Fig. 42 Marc Vellay and Kenneth Frampton, *Pierre Chareau: Architecte- meublier* (Paris: Editions
       du Regard, 1984) p. 268.
Fig. 43 William Howard Adams, *Jefferson's Monticello* (New York: Abbeville Press, 1983) p. 130.
Fig. 44 Bruno Zevi, p. 44.
Fig. 45 *Raffaello e L'Architettura a Firenze* (Firenze: Sansoni Editore, 1984) p. 192.
Fig. 46 Carpaccio, LA NASCITA DELLA VERGINE, Accademia Carrara (Bergamo, 1504-08).
Fig. 47 Shepard and Jellicoe, pl. 38, B [Retouched].
Fig. 48 Jean-Francois Pinchon, *Rob. Mallet — Stevens* (Paris: Action Artistique de Paris/Philippe
       Sers Editeur, 1986) p. 38.

PHOTOGRAPHY CREDITS

pp. 30-32   E. Alan McGee ©
p. 33   J. James Strange
p. 44   Anthony Ames
p. 45   J. James Strange
pp. 56-57   J. James Strange
pp. 70-71   Clark Tefft
pp. 86-99   Steven Brooke ©
pp. 116-129 Wayne N.P. Fujii ©

This book was printed and bound in the fall of 1987 by
Toppan Printing Co., Ltd., Japan
in an edition of 3,000 copies consisting of
1,000 clothbound, including 50 signed and numbered,
and 2,000 paperbound.
Typography by Action Graphics, Inc., Atlanta, Georgia.

133